BALANCE

Every Woman's Guide For Achieving A Stable And Fulfilling Life

Table of Contents

Introduction

Chapter 1: Understanding Balance

- Evaluating the concept of balance as it relates to a woman's life, demystifying the myths of balance, and putting in the right perspective, what balance really signifies.

Chapter 2: Seasons and Cycles

- Identifying seasons and cycles of a woman, guiding women to identify the different seasons of their lives and understand the essence of seasons and cycles better.

Chapter 3: Decipher your Seasons

- Determining the seasons of your life with clarity and providing practical tips on how to identify them.

Chapter 4: Make peace with your Seasons

- Providing women with practical tips for making peace with their seasons and maximizing the outcome of their lives, no matter what season of life they are in.

Chapter 5: Prioritizing the Demands of the Season:

- Identifying Priorities, navigating the landscape of priorities, and guiding women to identify and categorize their commitments, aspirations, and responsibilities. Tools and exercises to aid in evaluating and aligning these priorities to establish the foundation for a balanced life.

Chapter 6: Mastering the Act of Self-Management

- Unveiling effective self-management techniques and strategies tailored to a woman's lifestyle. This chapter focuses on practical tips, tools, and routines to optimize self-management and enhance productivity while fostering self-care and rejuvenation.

Chapter 7: Balancing Act

- Exploring the intricacies of balance, underscoring the requirements of balance on a day-to-day basis, and providing a practical guide to a balanced lifestyle, including fostering healthy relationships, whether personal, familial, or professional. Strategies for maintaining healthy boundaries, communication skills, and fostering meaningful connections are discussed.

Chapter 8: Integrating Life

- Achieving life integration, rather than compartmentalization, defining your goal for life integration, evaluating the resources available at your disposal in achieving life integration, and reviewing your current rhythm in a bid to improve them in a way that brings balance and fulfillment.

Chapter 9: Grit and Adaptability

- Coping with Change, examining the role of grit and adaptability in navigating life's inevitable changes, and Strategies for embracing change, overcoming setbacks, and leveraging challenges as opportunities for growth.

Chapter 10: Mindfulness and Present Living

- Exploring the transformative power of mindfulness in fostering balance. Techniques and practices are shared to help women cultivate present-moment awareness, reduce stress, and savor life's experiences.

Tieing everything Together

Acknowledgement

INTRODUCTION

In the whirlwind of modern life, and with several aspects of life screaming for attention, achieving balance could seem elusive, especially for women juggling multiple roles and responsibilities. A woman in this era often finds herself juggling several things: family, career, business, ministry, personal development as well as her spiritual, emotional, and mental wellbeing. How then can she navigate through all these very important areas of her life and still maintain balance? I have asked myself this very question on several occasions and have had many women walk up to me with the same question. On one particular occasion, I was speaking with a colleague about the many roles, responsibilities, and challenges that women in this era are facing in many facets of their lives and the various forces that drive the decisions they make which eventually, further shape their lives and those connected to them. One of the key things that have stood out from this conversation and in all the discussions I have had with many is the desire to achieve stability and balance. Many seek a life of familiarity, predictability, and control; a life where they can more reliably predict outcomes, feel more in charge of the

Introduction

happenings around them, and also feel more relaxed, less stressed and anxious, and just plainly enjoy comfort. Given the turbulence that has engulfed so many aspects of our world today which is further exacerbated by the unattainable expectation of society from women, it could seem that achieving stability and fulfillment is an uphill task.

In one of my recent engagements with women to find out how they juggle daily responsibilities, I met a woman in my daughter's school. I usually would drop my daughter off in the morning between 8:40 am and 8:50 am and just walk back home to continue with work. That morning, I just got into a quick chat with one of the mothers, and from there, we became friends. One of the days, she told me her story. She had graduated from school and gotten a job, and was doing prettywell in it; promotions were coming, life was good and there were no issues with balancing any area of her life. A few years later, she met her husband and got married. Life was still great until she got pregnant with her son and that season became too overwhelming for her; she was struggling to meet up both at work and at home front, she tried to stretch it through but at some point, her mental health got affected as well. Then, she had to choose between family and work. She had to step

Introduction

off work to be fully at home. Since then, she has now had more kids and has not been able to find the courage to go back to work. She said, "I would love to go back to work, but the stress of starting all over again just keeps me off completely, and I hope that someday, I'll find the courage once more to go back.

Her story parallels Karly's. Karly graduated from INSEAD Business School, brimming with enthusiasm and embracing the concept of "leaning in." She was fully committed to proving that she could achieve it all: excelling as a high-powered career woman while being a stellar mother. Initially, she managed this balancing act adeptly. However, after becoming a mother in 2018, she found herself shouldering the majority of childcare responsibilities. Her husband's frequent work-related travels as an architect meant that she had to step up. Despite maintaining her workload, she faced the added challenge of competing with male counterparts who didn't share her background struggles.

When Covid-19 struck, it seemed as though all the obstacles already impeding her progress were unleashed to the next level. Her daughter's school closed, thrusting her into the role of primary caregiver while trying to keep her head above water at work. She felt like she was constantly running on a treadmill, besieged from all directions.

Introduction

In early 2021, Karly's therapist diagnosed her with burnout. She merely scraped by each day, the initial energy and enthusiasm she possessed after graduation had completely dissipated.

These women's stories exemplify the plight of millions of women who grapple with navigating life and juggling the myriad responsibilities that accompany different stages of life. This work piece therefore is an attempt to provide a guiding compass, delving into strategies, insights, and perspectives tailored to help women create harmony, manage priorities, and nurture stability across various aspects of their lives.

These strategies, insights, and perspectives are designed to propel you to evaluate and improve balance in your life. It seeks to provide you with a clear picture of how you can determine the seasons of your life, assist you in identifying areas in which you might be undervaluing or overemphasizing, and enable you to focus on what matters in each season and truly enjoy those different seasons and components of your life. The reason for this evaluation is not to pass judgment or scrutinize your present status of balance but rather to act as a device for self-reflection and self-improvement. It will furnish

Introduction

you with a beginning stage for rolling out sure improvements and changes in your day-to-day existence which will lead to a better and really satisfying life.

Keep in mind that life balance is not tied to accomplishing flawlessness in each aspect of your life. It's about finding an agreeable mix that aligns with your values and needs. Join me as we navigate together in this journey to finding balance as a woman.

CHAPTER 1
UNDERSTANDING BALANCE

Balance is an individualistic concept that allows you to design your life in such a way as to ensure productive and happy living for different seasons

1. Understanding Balance

Many persons want balance without understanding what balance fully implies. To make it even more complicated is the fact that balance varies with different individuals, seasons, cultures, eras, and locations.

Balance is Individualistic

Balance is person-specific; it is not a one-size-fits-all thing. See, what signifies balance for one individual may put another in total disarray, hence, every woman must carry out a personal evaluation and determine what balance would mean to her. 'Woman A' may have a chain of activities that enable her to perform at her optimum which if implemented by 'Woman B' could completely throw her off course.

Balance Evolves with Seasons

Balance evolves with changes in seasons, even for the same individual. Seasons of our lives change even without our consent and sometimes, we are oblivious of it. So, it takes intentionality and mindful thinking to identify a change in season. A change in season will require a remodeling and redefining of what brings balance to your life. For example, a woman in her twenties might determine the actions, strategies, and activities that make up for her stability but if she fails to continuously evaluate her seasons and develop new sets of

1. Understanding Balance

activities and strategies that would enable her to adapt to the changing seasons of her life, she would find her life being out of course. That failure would not mean that she got the strategies wrong in her twenties, but it would be a result of failing to redefine and remodel the factors that contribute to her balance according to the changing seasons of her life and adopt a lifestyle and system that is commensurate with the changes.

As I contemplate the evolution of balance with the seasons of life, Anita Drozd's story quickly springs to mind. Anita had spent over 14 years working with the Polish Government in Kyiv before resigning to launch her own business, 'Youjuice'. Just prior to embarking on this entrepreneurial journey, she was doing quite well and had recently finished nursing a toddler. Although she started small, her business rapidly expanded from a single outlet to two additional locations, ultimately consuming her time. She toiled relentlessly, working seven days a week, enduring sleepless nights fraught with financial worries due to cash flow issues. Alongside this came the guilt of not allocating enough time for her child, partner, and friends. In her own words, "I felt totally overwhelmed, excited, and exhausted all at the same time."

1. Understanding Balance

A typical day for her would commence at 5 am. She planned every next day during a quick shower from the previous night and tackled unread emails over morning coffee and ginger drink. She juggled social media posts while preparing her daughter's packed lunch. At work, she pressed juice for eight to ten hours straight, all the while, fielding customers' life events and digestive issues, educating them about her products, and addressing operational challenges. Upon returning home, instead of resting, she plunged back into work to prepare for the following day. Despite feeling that she was neglecting vital commitments such as family trips and quality time with her daughter and partner, she reassured herself that she loved running the business, thus not overly concerned with taking time away from it.

She was busy and incredibly popular. However, somewhere between opening the second and third outlet, her marriage disintegrated. Suddenly, customers began spending less money, leading to frustration, sleep deprivation, and mental exhaustion for Anita. By April 2017, she found herself unable to effectively communicate with her team. With no other option, she decided to temporarily shut down the business.

1. Understanding Balance

Three weeks of reflection and evaluation revealed to her that she desperately needed a change. The seasons of her life had shifted, but she hadn't adjusted her strategies accordingly. She had allowed one aspect of her life to overshadow all others. She realized that she needed to define what happiness and balance meant for herself and her loved ones. For Anita, balance should have meant pursuing her passion without sacrificing her presence in her daughter's life. It should have meant finding time to exercise each morning and stepping away from the business when necessary.

Balance Differs with Culture and Era

Culture plays a key role in shaping different individuals across the globe. Culture affects how we think about ourselves and others, how we represent ourselves, and what we achieve in our work and lives. Culture, specifically, family culture somehow shapes how we define and even achieve balance. A woman who finds herself in a culture that values family togetherness, a culture where family members are more out to provide a support system, will see balance differently from a woman who lives in a culture that hardly promotes such.

1. Understanding Balance

A woman living in a culture where women are expected to be responsible for things that men in that cultural context are not expected to do will naturally not be able to feel a sense of balance when she is not meeting those expectations. Besides the pressure from society, she will unconsciously include those expectations as part of her goal of achieving balance.

Achieving balance has evolved with different eras. What could seem like a level of balance for women who were born in the 90s will totally differ from what those born in the twenty-first Century view in the same light. Women in the 90s obviously had their own challenges, however, these challenges are significantly different from the challenges faced by women in this current generation. Women in the 90s were more likely to celebrate staying at home to take care of their families than the women of this era would. Women in the 90s didn't have to deal with pressures from social media, to fit into a certain lifestyle acceptable on those platforms. A Woman in this dispensation, aside from societal pressure, wants to be more for herself and this goes a long way in determining what she terms as being successful. Women in this current era are grappling with a barrage of responsibilities ranging from wanting to be heard, leading in the workplace, making societal impacts, raising

1. Understanding Balance

responsible children, and nurturing them into successful adults, keeping the home front together, as well as keeping physically and mentally fit. Coupled with all of these, she must deal with the ever-changing technology at her disposal.

A combined consideration of all these factors as stated above must be considered and refined and put into perspective to be able to arrive at what balance really means to you as a woman. In crafting your balance strategy, you must consider your personal needs, seasons, and culture, as well as the peculiarities of your environment and consciously evaluate and refine them as you go along your life journey.

It is worth noting that balance in the context of a woman's life has been massively misconstrued over the years. This misconception differs across society, ages, and eras across different societal demography. What are some of these misconceptions?

Balance-Means-Perfection Misconception

To achieve balance does not mean that everything has to be perfect. Many women struggle to achieve perfection in all areas of their lives at the same time. They feel that to achieve balance, everything has to be perfect, and every area of their lives has to be working optimally at the same rate and at the

1. Understanding Balance

same time every day. However, regardless of how diligently you attempt, there will be times when some areas of your life will not be prim and proper. Your ability to achieve perfection in all areas of your life at the same rate and at the same time is limited. The realization that there will be days you will achieve perfection, days when every one of your plans will go according to the script, and also, days when it will not, will free up your mind and release more energy and ability to focus on what you have control over and enjoy a more fruitful and fulfilling life. As much as you strive to achieve perfection, understand that it's okay to have an imperfect day and still have a balanced life.

Balance-Means-Uniform-Engagement Misconception

There is also the misconception that balance is achieved when there is an equal investment of time in all the important aspects of life. Achieving balance is not about giving equal time and energy to each area of life. Rather, it's about giving the right portion to different areas of your life, and this will differ on different days. There are days when it will be 100% work, there are days when it might be 100% childcare, days of 100% self-care, and days when it will be a mix of different areas of your life. Different days will require dynamic trade-offs. There is no

1. Understanding Balance

static proportion to give you balance, the key lies in evaluating your peculiar situation and prioritizing according to your changing needs.

The Superwoman Misconstruction

This is the misconstruction that a superwoman is a woman who has it all in, a successful career, bubbling social life, perfect family, and social influence, all simultaneously without some level of trade-offs and a support system. A superwoman is being misconstrued to do everything all by herself. However, this is but a mirage as it's unattainable to have it all in at the same time and by yourself. This has made many women live in pretense and put up a front that they have it all in. This prevents them from taking steps to achieve real balance. There will be seasons and days when you will not have it all in, and there will be seasons of challenges and sacrifice in one of those areas in order to establish progress in other areas. There will be times and occasions when you will need support systems and that will neither make you less of a superwoman nor mean that your life is out of balance.

Balance-Means-Neglecting-Selfcare Misconception

Many women think that considering themselves last and taking care of everyone and everything else first gives the required

1. Understanding Balance

satisfaction that makes for balance. This spans from the natural tendency of a woman to want to take care of everyone and everything. A woman will consider her family, her boss, her career, society, etc before even considering herself. Have you ever gone to the supermarket and thought, "This will be a good fit for so and so", and then at the end of it, you found out that you spent the least on your needs? Yes, that is what I'm talking about. Can you think of the times when you have felt dizzy and not feeling your whole body, yet you pushed on to take care of your children's needs and even wants, or can you think about when you have felt so unwell, yet you pushed on to deliver on a tight deadline and please your boss? Yes, that's what I'm talking about. You need to realize that as a woman, you need to be whole within and without to be able to effectively achieve any level of balance around you. There will be times when you push beyond and above, but you should know when to recharge, when to seek help, when to say 'no' to others, and prioritize your well-being because in there lies your balance.

The Assumption that balance is one-size-fits-all

Nothing can be off the mark than the assumption that balance is the same for all women. There is a misconception that what signifies balance to one woman will be the same for all women.

1. Understanding Balance

However, this is far from the truth. Balance will vary from one individual to the other and in different seasons and circumstances.

The Misconception that Balance comes from Compartmentalized Living

Another fantasy is that balance comes with the compartmentalization of life. For some of us, that implies an even 50-50 split where we invest equal time and energy in different areas of our lives. For others, it's about dividing our days into 8-8-8 hours. This longstanding mindset suggests that we should spend eight hours at work, another eight hours resting, and reserve eight hours for relaxation, social activities, exercise, and family. For many, it means segregating the entirety of their being into different compartments. While compartmentalization helps organize life, it's essential to approach it with the understanding that life is interconnected, and all these compartments are integrated with each other. I can't begin to count the number of times I've had to send emails from a hospital hallway because I'm at work but need to make a hospital appointment for my children or send an mail while commuting from school runs. There are also times when I've had to reduce time with family because of work or a self-

1. Understanding Balance

development program. There have also been seasons of my life when I've had to adjust the 8-8-8-hour model because a project needed completion and days when I needed more rest to recover from a prolonged period of insufficient sleep.

Instead of forcing yourself to compartmentalize your life, allocate the appropriate amount of time to your current needs. For instance, when facing a work deadline, you may need to devote more time than usual to work, which may result in less time for other areas. Once that task is accomplished, you can then dedicate more time to being with your loved ones or even celebrate with them with a getaway.

The Balance-means-having-everything Misconception

There is also the misconceived idea that balance is about having it all. This is far from true. There are seasons when you have to shed some weight, let go of some friendships, not have sufficient time for family, and won't pursue promotion at the workplace because there is an urgent and important family need to meet. Again, it all boils down to the current season and the priority of the moment.

Try not to fall into the trap of thinking that you can have everything or do all that you desire. Sometimes, you need to sacrifice specific things while pursuing your goals and

1. Understanding Balance

dreams. The sooner you realize this, the quicker you'll be able to eliminate the unnecessary from your life until you've reached your goal.

Having explored the misconceptions of balance, what then is Balance?

Balance is an individualistic concept that allows you to design your life in such a way as to ensure productive and happy living for different seasons. At its core, balance is simply thinking about the various aspects of your life, how they interact, and how you'd like them to interact for more happiness and less stress as you live through different seasons.

Let's begin to explore the benefits you will enjoy when you have balance as a woman.

Guilt-free Life:

There is a freedom that comes with knowing that your life is operating at its optimum given the resources available to you. By this, I'm not talking about lacking aspiration and staying constantly on the path of least resistance, no. I'm talking about the peace, the serenity you enjoy knowing that you are doing what is best for the different aspects that make up your being. That is what balance brings. Many women

1. Understanding Balance

constantly live in that guilt zone, thinking they could have given more to their family in a season they are giving more to work or any other area of their life. However, understanding that you are operating at your optimum removes such guilt and frees up more energy to prosecute your life in its entirety.

Soundness of Mind:

With guilt stripped away, comes a sound mind. A balanced life will produce a sound mind. Balance brings about peace within, which will, in turn, produce a sound mind.

Overall Health:

Achieving balance as a woman will boost your overall health, leaving you better prepared for a more fulfilling life. Not having balance in your life as a woman leaves you stressed and, in the long run, could lead to a damaged health.

Increased Productivity:

Balancing different elements of life allows for more attention, energy, and efficiency in all areas of life. A woman who has built balance amongst several interconnected areas of her life has definitely created a system within and without that allows her to be productive.

1. Understanding Balance

Better Relationships:

It promotes better connections with family, friends, and colleagues by allocating time and attention to these interactions. Additionally, by defining what balance means for you in different seasons and stages of life, you are able to avoid overcommitment; you will be more intentional with your relationships and foster only the relationships that matter to your overall purpose.

Enhanced Self-Presence and Awareness:

Many women float through the seasons of their lives; they passively watch days, months, and years pass by. Balance brings you into active involvement with your seasons. It enables you to better understand your needs, strengths, and limitations, resulting in enhanced self-awareness/presence and self-esteem that allows you to actively engage your strengths and outsource your areas of weakness and limitations.

Fulfillment:

The hallmark of a balanced life is fulfillment. Balance allows you to follow your passions, hobbies, and personal ambitions and visions while meeting your obligations, resulting in a more rewarding existence.

1. Understanding Balance

Chapter Exercise:

Take up a pen and paper or whatever writing material you have and evaluate your own life by answering these questions:

1. What season of my life am I in now?
2. What are the basic needs of this season?
3. What would balance mean for me in this season?

CHAPTER TWO
SEASONS AND CYCLES

Everything happening in our lives happens in seasons

2. Seasons and Cycles

One of the constant things on Earth is seasons and cycles. The entire Earth functions in seasons and cycles, and each season differs completely from the other, according to each geographical region. For example, in Africa, with Nigeria as a case study, you will basically find two major seasons: the rainy season and the dry season. The extent of these two seasons varies across the different landscapes of the nation and across the different states that make up the nation. The annual precipitation ranges from anything below 20 inches in the North to as much as 120 inches in the extreme South. Each year, the level of this season could be different; in some years, you could get a mild rainy season, while in some years, it could be so rainy that you feel like the entire ocean wants to empty itself on the earth.

In some other regions like England and other European countries, there are four major seasons: Summer, Winter, Spring, and Autumn. Each of these seasons is different, each with its own beauty and challenges. And as far as the Earth remains, seasons and cycles will always remain. People come and go, politicians and policies come and go, but one thing that remains

2. Seasons and Cycles

constant is the cycle of seasons and times. Every year, there will always be summer, winter, spring, and autumn; the level of the extremity of these seasons could differ every year and in different places. Some winters could get so extreme; others could be mild, but the fact remains that it always comes, and it has a time it will end within the year.

Governments and individuals have learned to work with seasons. While some are better prepared and adapted for it, others float through the seasons. Many people have built systems that enable them to navigate through those seasons and times, while others just wait for the season to come and then, just watch it pass without maximizing the beauty of that season to their advantage.

In the same way nations and regions experience seasons, our lives as women go through seasons and cycles. Everything happening in our lives happens in seasons. There is a season to give birth, seasons to plant, seasons of harvest, seasons of coming together and partnering with others, and seasons to stay away from others and walk alone to build in some things within. There will be seasons to build connections and

2. Seasons and Cycles

relationships and other seasons to give up on certain relationships and connections that are no longer serving the required purpose. There will be seasons of pain, and there will certainly be seasons to heal from those pains. There will be seasons when you will fight your way through life, but there will also be seasons when you peacefully and calmly walk into opportunities you didn't plan for. These are all seasons; however, broadly speaking, and for our discussion, a woman's life will go through two categories of seasons: recurrent and non-recurrent seasons.

Non-Recurrent seasons

These are the seasons of life that occur with aging. The subject of aging is one that many women shy away from discussing; however, its reality stares at us with each passing day. They are non-recurrent because once that stage of life is gone, it cannot repeat itself. As much as a woman in her sixties would want to be sweet sixteen, she cannot; her bones and general body systems will always remind her otherwise. The non-recurrent seasons covered here include:

2. Seasons and Cycles

Season one: Young Woman

This is the season between teenage age and mid-twenties. It is the stage of life when most of our lives start. This stage begins with puberty, with the body building its hormones, and the girl-child beginning to develop into an adult. This season comes with a desire to experiment and explore the details of life; a stage where you are carefree and take as many risks as possible. This season of life comes with a lot of education and formative training, both formal and informal. It is at this stage that some values and principles begin to form, either consciously or unconsciously. This season creates the springboard on which other seasons of life kicks off. This is the period when the young woman is unconsciously influenced by parents, peers, society, and culture. At this season, her ideologies of life are shaped by these influences. Also, at this stage of life, the young woman wants to leave home and escape from being told what to do by her parents. She wants to be her own woman.

2. Seasons and Cycles

Season Two: Grown Woman

Gradually, she transitions from the season of a young woman to the season of a growing woman and eventually a grown woman. This season is a period of full responsibility; many women would have left home. It takes place between mid-twenties and late forties and is characterized by juggling many things in life. Women in this season juggle between making choices of a life partner, getting married, finding a career path, choosing to raise kids, building successful businesses, making societal impacts, and trying to find the perfect blend of all that gives them the highest level of fulfillment. With so many demands, it's natural to expect a lot from your body, and the good news for us is that at this stage of life, our bodies, and minds spirits are at their peak and could be maximized to efficiently handle so much. Your muscle mass and bone density have never been stronger than they would become at this stage.

As bright as this season is, it could become easy to be trapped in routines and societal expectations of what your life should be. At this stage of life, it becomes critical for a woman to discover who she wants to

2. Seasons and Cycles

become and proactively work on becoming that, rather than following a pattern. This is the season where she begins to build a legacy, find purpose, and live it out to the fullest. It is the stage of life where a woman is most energized by nature and can take on many ventures, set objectives, and achieve them.

Season three: Mature Woman

This is the season when most women begin to live out their lives. It's not a season of uncertainty and experimentation; rather, it's a time when a woman is supposed to know what she wants. At this stage, she has been taught through training, experiences, exposure, and challenges. She is more reflective, more aware, and more mature than before. She is better equipped to handle problems and challenges. It is the stage for correcting errors of the past and mentoring others based on experiences. For some women, it could be a season of realization. Some suddenly discover that what they have become is not what they inwardly want to be. Some begin to realize that they did not take some risks they should have taken in earlier years, and they try to correct their errors. Some may be fortunate enough to

2. Seasons and Cycles

take corrective measures, while others, unfortunately, are not able to due to health, strength, or lack of resources.

Season Four: Reclined Woman

This is the last season of a woman's life as far as the aging cycle is concerned. Not much can be done at this stage of life. What remains are memories of what has been achieved in the other three seasons of life. At this stage, muscles, nerves, and bones begin to give way and certain things that brought satisfaction in earlier seasons may not make as much sense. Some women may not be fortunate enough to reach this stage of life. Many at this stage are already grandmothers and great-grandmothers.

See, these four seasons do not reoccur; you have one time to live out each of them. Hence, what you do with these four seasons is much more important than simply knowing that they exist. I have seen reclined women who were once young women, who lived bustling and reckless lives, now having only memories of what they could have done better. The nature of these seasons is that they can never be repeated. I have also seen women

2. Seasons and Cycles

in their matured stage take corrective measures and were able to fulfill more purpose than some who have the strength and natural resources on their side but are currently wasting them away.

The Recurring or Cyclical Seasons

These are seasons that are cyclical or recurring in nature; they do not happen just once in a lifetime. They are not static; at certain times in your life, they can happen more than once. The length of time they take also differs; it could be a few months or it can stretch into years depending on when they have played out their full course and achieved their purpose. These seasons, without a proper understanding, could be taking place in a person's life, and the person would be completely oblivious to what is going on. They require discernment and intentionality to discover and maximize their potential to create balance in your life. What are these recurring/cyclical seasons?

Season of Preparation

The season of preparation is like setting the stage for the artist to perform. A lot goes on behind the scenes; it's a stage of life where you are not seen. It's a season of

2. Seasons and Cycles

personal development and transformation. Sometimes in your season of preparation, you are not even aware of what you are being prepared for, but all you know is that the experiences, training, and exposures seem to be geared towards a particular direction. It's like the imaginary woman being prepared to be a queen. At the time of that preparation, she was not aware of what she was being prepared for. All she knew was that she was being trained to walk in a particular way. She was not to associate and play like other young girls of her age. While her age mates could risk getting drunk, she could not even taste anything alcoholic. While her age mates could get three square meals a day, she could not. Her age mates could dress in certain ways, but for her, she couldn't, not because she was being forced not to do these things, but because an instinct kept her from doing them. Even when she tried once or twice to follow these norms, she felt no pleasure in them. While these may seem extreme, at different times and in different areas of our lives, we are constantly going through seasons of preparation for what comes next. Like what happens before the planting season, the soil and the seed get

2. Seasons and Cycles

prepared; there will be clearing, decluttering, and tilling. In some other season of preparation, you are certain; you are aware of what you are being trained for. This season could happen in your ministry, your marriage, your career, etc. It may not happen all at the same time in all areas of your life. You may be in a season of preparation in your career and in a totally different season in your marriage. A season of preparation could be a time of intense training, practice, experimentation, seeming failures, and learning from those failures. A season of preparation is a season when your character is tested, your strength and resolve go through the fire, and the integrity of the material you are building your life, career, marriage, and business is tested. Also, your values and principles are tested in this season. The season of preparation can be challenging, but if you persevere long enough to go through it, it could produce the highest level of transformation you never imagined. It could be dark in the tunnel of preparation, but if you can patiently go through it and allow it to shape you, you will come out stronger,

2. Seasons and Cycles

healthier, more mature, and better equipped for what you have been prepared for.

Season of Planting

Relatable to the planting season in farming, the planting season of our lives is the time to sow new seeds. Once the season of preparation is done, the next season is the season of planting. The planting season is the season for new things; a time to step into new terrains and a time to do things you have not done before. The planting season could be a time to step up and take a new level of challenge in your marriage, career, business, and circle of influence. If you thought that the preparation season was tough, the planting season can be scary. As human beings, we usually get comfortable with routine and what we have done in the past. It takes courage to step out of the familiar into the unknown. Our imaginary lady who was being prepared to be a queen, who at the time didn't know would have her head buzzing with thoughts when the time came for the selection of a new queen. She must have had a thousand and one thoughts telling her that she was not enough. Everything within her told her not to compete. Her clothing was not

2. Seasons and Cycles

flamboyant enough, her looks were not perfect for a queen, and her speech was not the speech of a queen. She must have told herself that she had been malnourished from not eating the right number of meals. She was not as pretty as most girls raised in wealthy homes, so why try at all? She would have been confronted with the fear of "what if she was not selected?" All these factors were real to her, but she faced her fears and contested anyways.

This season requires boldness to shove your fears and make those bold steps irrespective of them. In the planting season, a seed is taken and sowed into the soil. At the time of putting the seed in the soil, the Sower is not certain that it will grow, some of the seed sown may not even germinate, but others will. Some may yield more results than others, but the focus is that something has been planted. In your season of planting, be deliberate in planting the right seeds, be deliberate in making those connections and relevant relationships. Be deliberate in your career to speak up on the skills and experiences you have, be deliberate in speaking about your business, be deliberate in speaking about your

2. Seasons and Cycles

visions and aspirations, and be intentional in making that career shift. Maybe you are not sure how it will turn out but do it despite your fears, doubts, and lack of resources. Apply for that job, raise your family, and do something new with your business, because you know what, you have been equipped for it. You have been prepared for such a time as this. Not all the new things you try will work out as planned. When you raise your hand to take on new responsibilities in your office, it's not all the time that you may be allowed to do it, but you have sown a seed that says, "I am responsible, I can be trusted to do this", you have been taken note of. Scatter your seeds in this season as much as possible, some will yield thirty folds, others sixty, and others hundred folds. You don't lose when you plant, you lose if you don't plant at all.

Season of Hibernating/Waiting

The season of Hibernation or waiting is the lag between the season of planting and the season of harvest. Some waiting can be days, weeks, months, or even years. A woman who wants balance must exercise patience and calmness during the season of waiting. It is this season that some run out of patience and get frustrated. In the waiting season, try as much as possible to take your rest and practice self-care. The first two seasons have taken a lot of your energy; as such, you will need to refresh and get re-energized because the next season could be quite hectic. Have fun during this time, develop new hobbies, and do something relaxing.

Season of Harvest

The season of harvest is the season of results. It's the season when you are on the stage, the season when you move from being on the backstage to being on the platform. At this stage, most people will begin to wonder how you got to where you are, they are not aware of the other three seasons you have had to go through. They are not aware of the preparation season, the long nights of study, the long days of workout, the number of hours it took to practice, the number of days with no food, the number of times you had to put the extra hours into that career, business, ministry, and marriage. They are not aware of the sacrifices made; all they can see in this season is the glory. It can be a busy

2. Seasons and Cycles

period, but very rewarding. At this season, your efforts are rewarded, and your every step is noticed.

Why Do Seasons Happen?

You are reading this book right now and you are wondering to yourself, "Why do seasons happen in our lives as women? Why do I have to go through seasons?" Here are some of the reasons.

Seasons happen to keep you focused on certain things within a given time. You don't have all the time in the world to be doing everything simultaneously. You cannot be preparing for an Olympics for the first time, and at the same time be the champion in the same game you are practicing for. Seasons are systems that allow you to focus on certain things within a specific period. Seasons happen to change you; they aim at changing you because when you go through certain seasons of life, you are being transformed both within. Notice the word, 'when' because seasons are constant but aim at transforming you into an adaptable woman. If there were no seasons, life would be very stagnant. Can you imagine a world where everything remains static? I could bet it would be boring. Seasons happen to give

2. Seasons and Cycles

you diverse experiences. Imagine an earth where it is all summer; maybe the temperature will get so hot and everything will die, or can you imagine an earth where it is all winter, maybe, all living things will die off from frost. Therefore, seasons bring balance to the earth and give us diverse experiences. Seasons come with an inbuilt beauty and challenges thereby exposing us to varying experiences. Can you imagine a world where everything remains static? I bet it would be boring. Seasons happen to allow you time to reset. Imagine a life where everything is active all at the same time; our human mind and system will shut down. Seasons allow us to reset and recalibrate when things are quieter in our lives. Seasons happen to take away what is not needed and replace it with what is required. Seasons help us to evaluate and take away that which is not needed for what is required in our journey to achieving purpose. Someone once told a story of a time in their city when the winter didn't get to be as cold as was required and did not last for a long time and the next spring, there were so many bugs everywhere. This was because the bite of the winter didn't get intense enough to kill the

2. Seasons and Cycles

bugs, so in the spring, when the temperature got higher, they all spread out everywhere. Certain seasons of our lives happen because some mindsets need to be dealt with, and some friendships need to go. Some habits need to be dealt with. Seasons are important to fixing us and fixing the conditions around us in readiness for who and where we need to be.

Chapter Exercise

Now that you know about the seasons, can you ask yourself these questions?

1. What season of my life have I missed or not maximized?
2. What steps do I need to take to maximize my current season?
3. How do I determine what season I am in so that I will maximize my life and achieve my goals?

CHAPTER THREE
DECIPHER YOUR SEASONS

For a woman who wants to achieve balance, you will need to be able to decipher the seasons of your life in different areas to achieve balance and fulfillment

3. Decipher your seasons

Now that you are aware of the seasons, you may be wondering: "How do I know what season of life I'm in?" The non-recurrent seasons are much easier to determine. In fact, most people are aware of the non-recurrent seasons but find it difficult to do what needs to be done during those seasons. Hence, our focus in this chapter is on the seasons that are not easy to determine: the recurrent seasons.

When seasons change in nature, we do not see the season; we cannot touch it. But there are certain features that we see, feel, and test, and we say that the season has changed. For a woman who wants to achieve balance, you will need to be able to decipher the seasons of your life in different areas to achieve balance and fulfillment. In the previous chapters, we talked about four seasons: The seasons of preparation, planting, waiting, and harvest. Here are the things that will let you know that you are in any of these seasons:

Preparation Season

Discomfort with the status quo: Mostly, the season of preparation begins with discomfort with the status quo. The things that you originally enjoyed doing, you

3. Decipher your seasons

suddenly lose interest in. The way you worked and had no issues with in the past, you just find out that you are no longer satisfied with them. The season of preparation can demand a level of separation. For some of the relationships you kept in the past, you'll suddenly discover that you no longer feel the need to hang around these people anymore. When you see these signs, they indicate that you are stepping into a season of preparation.

Heightened Inquisitiveness: The season of preparation comes with a high level of inquisitiveness. It's a season where you begin to question a lot of things. You are questioning why certain things have been done in certain ways and why they cannot be done another way. You begin to question processes and systems you didn't blink an eye about previously.

Strong desire for knowledge and growth: With that inquisitiveness comes a strong desire for knowledge and growth. The season of preparation comes with an unquenchable hunger for knowledge and growth. You will no longer just be asking questions, but you will also be searching for knowledge to solve the problems being

3. Decipher your seasons

inquired about. These desires will make you go the extra mile to take the necessary training.

Unusual strength: The season of preparation comes with a lot of mental, spiritual, and emotional stress, and at the same time, it supplies the needed strength required to go through it if only you can reach out within and to your source for the strength required for that season. I have had to go through many seasons of preparation in my own life, and after each of them, I was curious about how I mustered the strength to go through all of them without breaking down. That is what the season of preparation does. In the season of preparation, you can withstand what tears others down.

Lack of Opportunities: When you are in a season of preparation, and you are seeking an opportunity to perform the same things you are being trained for, those opportunities will not open. Have you ever had an experience where you felt that you already know some things and you are trying to get into certain leagues of some key players in that field and they are not opening up? It is because you are in your season of preparation. Maybe in your business, career, or other areas of life,

3. Decipher your seasons

you are trying to get into certain terrains, but seem not to be making headway. Could it be that you have not elapsed your season of preparation? When opportunities are not opening, go back and train more, rather than grumble and want to jump the process. Go back and sharpen those skills. Maybe in your quest for knowledge, you might even create opportunities for others to tap into.

Planting Season

Strong desire to launch out: The planting season is characterized by a strong desire to launch out: you have been preparing for something in certain areas of your life, and suddenly, there is an instinctive strong desire to launch out. This right here is your planting season. It does not stem from a desire to just show off what you have learned; rather, it comes from the place of knowing from within that it's the right thing to do at that time. Each time you want to sit back and continue learning and preparing, you will no longer feel that satisfaction anymore. This is the time to launch out, this is the time to plant. It is time to make that application, it is time to write that business proposal and bring your idea to life,

3. Decipher your seasons

it is time to write that book; it is the time you have been preparing for all along. You may still have doubts and fears, but the desire to launch out will be stronger if only you will maximize this time and do it irrespective of the negative feelings.

A strong desire to Speak out: The season of planting brings with it a strong desire to speak out about your skills, abilities, and experiences. It is in your planting season that you receive the strength to take on a challenging project, something you have not tried before in your office, in your business, or your marriage. It is in this season that there will be a welling up within to talk about what you know without fear. Some women know that they have this desire to speak about something they have spent lots of time and investment privately learning about, but because of the lack of understanding of their season, they go back and bottle it in. This is not the time to keep shut; speak up, be your own magnifying glass, talk about how you have overcome the risks, and the experiences you have gathered in your preparation season, maximize this season, and see how far your seed can travel!

3. Decipher your seasons

A strong desire to expand what you do: In the preparation season, you may be satisfied with having it small, but with the planting season, there is a strong desire to expand, to go big. The planting season is the season to scatter your seeds far and wide and as deep as possible. The problem for some people is that they have been in the season of preparation for so long, and when the time for planting came, they talked themselves back into their shell, into that small corner, and rather than expand, they remained in that season of smallness and the season of preparation that had long expired. Once there is that desire to launch out and expand, do not kill it, maximize it and expand. You may make some mistakes along the way; you may get some "no's" along your path, bring in your A, B, and C game but don't run back to smallness.

Resources for Planting show up: This right here is very important; sometimes what marks the end of your preparation season is the seed to plant. There will be no planting season for a farmer if there are no seeds to plant, relatedly what marks the end of the planting season would be the seed to plant. Your seed could be a

3. Decipher your seasons

new business idea that suddenly shows up, a new grant to start up that business, a new loan, an accumulation of savings you were putting away for your idea, a new career opportunity, and an opening in companies you had always wanted to work with, it could be anything. You need to be discerning to know that this is your seed, this is your resource, this is your opportunity, don't kill or eat it and wait endlessly. Many women have eaten their seed thinking that it's the harvest. Don't let that happen to you.

The Waiting Season

It's a quiet season: The waiting or hibernation season is usually very quiet, it's that season where it seems like your life has suddenly come to a standstill. When this happens, know that this is your waiting season. Many times, after you have sown the seed, and it seems like nothing is happening, it's probably your waiting season. Patience is required in this season because it's probably the season when your seed is running deep into the soil to bring the type of result commensurate with your level of preparation.

3. Decipher your seasons

A strong desire to rest and refresh: The waiting season usually comes with a strong desire to take some rest, refresh, and re-strategize. Don't waste this season; it may not seem as important as the others but it's very crucial. If you miss this season, if you waste it by getting sad and stressing yourself, you may experience burnout when the next season arrives.

Harvest Season

Diverse opportunities open: The season of harvest is characterized by diverse opportunities. In this season, you get multiple offers and many people partnering with you. Maximize those opportunities.

Ease of connection: In the season of harvest, you will find it easier to connect with people. You will not do so much for people to want to identify with you. In the season of harvest, people will go out of their way to introduce you to useful connections and introduce your products, services, and skills.

Little actions, great results: In the season of harvest, every little step, every little action you take, produces maximally. The places that may have rejected you in the season of preparation, come for you. The little things

3. Decipher your seasons

you did before that didn't reward you in the past, you might want to try again this season and ride on the wave of the season for maximum results and rewards.

Heightened performance: In the season of harvest, you perform at your best. The season of harvest comes with pronounced results. In this season, the impact of your products and services will be felt and greatly maximized.

Now that we have talked about how you can decipher the seasons of your life by checking the prominent experiences and instincts within, it is worthy of note to mention that different areas of your life may not necessarily be in the same season at the same time. This is very key for balance. Your marriage could be at the preparation season while your career might be at the planting or harvest season. Knowing what to do for each area going through its own cycle of seasons is paramount to enjoying balance and fulfillment. See you in the next chapters as we delve in more, before then take some moment to perform this chapter exercise.

3. Decipher your seasons

Chapter Exercise:

Now that you know what to look out for in any season, can you perform this exercise?

1. What characterizes my current season? You can outline different areas of your life and measure them against the characteristics we have highlighted in this chapter.
2. How do I maximize the season in each of these areas

CHAPTER FOUR
MAKE PEACE WITH YOUR SEASONS.

Balance doesn't just come from knowing your seasons; it starts with acknowledging and making peace with the seasons of your life. Making peace with your season means reaching a place of acceptance and joy, irrespective of the challenges and demands of that season

4. Make peace with your seasons

Growing up in Africa (Nigeria), we had two major seasons - rainy and dry seasons. I enjoyed these two seasons and adapted to them so well that I hardly noticed when the seasons changed. Each season had its enjoyable aspects, but there was always something I found challenging. During the dry season, I could appreciate the cozy breeze of Harmattan but disliked the intense heat, profuse sweating, and dried and cracked lips. In the rainy season, I enjoyed the moderate temperature and the calmness the rains brought. As a child, my siblings and I loved playing in the rain. However, some rainy seasons could be extreme, with heavy rains disrupting my movements, which I found unpleasant.

Moving to the United Kingdom, I finally experienced white Christmases and real autumn foliage. Initially, the thoughts of seeing the entire street covered in snow, everything turning white in winter, and the leaves falling off in autumn were appealing to my mind. However, during my first Christmas here, while excited about the snow, the frost sent shivers down my spine with each walk on the street, converting an envisaged

4. Make peace with your seasons

paradise into a trauma. I dreaded walking outside and preferred staying indoors, wrapped up, and watching the streets through the windows. When spring finally arrived, it was a relief; it was gorgeous, exhilarating, and relaxing. As I adjusted to the seasons, summer followed with its high temperatures, resembling those of my home country but with lower humidity, longer days, and shorter nights. I found it fascinating that the sun could still be up at 10 p.m., and bright even at 5 a.m. Then autumn came with all the leaves turning brown, which was exciting to watch and experience. Living through these seasons was both exhilarating and mind-boggling; realizing how different places and regions could experience varying seasons simultaneously.

In the next winter, I made some adjustments both in my mindset and disposition. Not because it was no longer chilly and snowy, but because I had changed. I had shifted my mindset, adjusted my approach, and accepted the seasons. I no longer dreaded walking in the snow, and I even found joy in working and writing in the dark. Just as seasons occur in nature, they also happen in our lives. Sometimes, we are aware of these

4. Make peace with your seasons

seasons but fail to leverage the advantages they bring, merely going through them without yielding the desired results.

Balance doesn't just come from knowing your seasons; it starts with acknowledging and making peace with the seasons of your life. Making peace with your season means reaching a place of acceptance and joy, irrespective of the challenges and demands of that season. How then does a woman going through the seasons of her life find peace with them?

Focus on the Season!

Often, when we lose peace with a season, it's because we lost focus on it. We become preoccupied with the next season of our lives, failing to maximize the benefits and great things happening in our current season. I remember when I got my first job, I was more concerned about the next job, the next role, and the next big thing in my life, failing to recognize the opportunities and joys of my current season. Similarly, whether you're a single woman worrying about marriage or a married woman in a career-building

4. Make peace with your seasons

season, focus on the benefits and growth opportunities of your current season while planning for the next.

Be joyful in all seasons

Joy isn't dependent on external circumstances; it comes from within and can be cultivated. Choosing to be joyful in every season provides the strength to endure challenges and appreciate the beauty of each season's lessons and experiences.

Be thankful for all seasons

Every season has its beauty and purpose, whether it's a season of growth, challenges, or transitions. Instead of complaining, embrace each season with gratitude, recognizing the lessons and growth it brings.

Embrace the demands of the season

Accepting and embracing the unique challenges and opportunities of each season is crucial for finding balance and fulfillment. Rather than resisting or denying the season you're in, proactively engage with it and seek support when needed.

Go with the pace of the season

Recognize that each season has its rhythm and flow. Trying to rush through or resist the natural pace of a

4. Make peace with your seasons

season can lead to frustration and dissatisfaction. Embrace the pace of each season, knowing that it serves a purpose in your overall journey.

Avoid the temptation of comparison

Comparing your life to others can lead to discontent and rob you of joy in your current season. Celebrate others' successes but focus on your own journey and growth, recognizing that everyone's seasons are different.

Engage with the season

Actively participate in the lessons and experiences of each season, seeking to learn and grow from them. Be present and open-minded, recognizing that each season has something to teach you.

Do not be fearful of the season

Fear can hinder your ability to embrace and fully experience the season you're in. Instead of succumbing to fear, boldly face the challenges and opportunities of each season, knowing that you have the strength to overcome them.

Chapter Exercise

Reflect on the following questions and write down your answers.

4. Make peace with your seasons

1. Have I made peace with my current season?

2. What barriers have prevented me from making peace with my season?

3. How can I resolve these barriers?

CHAPTER FIVE
PRIORITIZE THE DEMANDS OF YOUR SEASON

Each shifting Season has its demand as such prioritizing the demands of each season is key if you are to experience a fulfilling life of balance

5. Prioritize the demands of your season

The realization that you are just one person, with multiple facets of life, and that there will not be enough time, energy, financial, and other resources to do everything means that you will need to set priorities for your life. Additionally, you will have different experiences for the different seasons of your life; as such, your priorities must shift with the changing seasons. Therefore, prioritizing the demands of each season is key if you are to experience a fulfilling life of balance. How then can you prioritize the demands of your season?

Determine the most important things for every season of your life.

It is important that as you go through your seasons, you ask yourself, "What are the critical things I need to do in this season?" Let's take, for example, your marriage. Like most other areas of life, marriages, as we discussed, go through four seasons: the season of preparations, the season of planting, the season of waiting, and the season of harvest. The season of preparation in your marriage could be the season when you are learning, trying to understand your spouse, the

5. Prioritize the demands of your season

terrain of marriage, and the best possible ways to make it work and fit into your overall vision as a person. The season of planting may be those seasons of raising your kids, and giving love and affection to your spouse and children, to mention but a few. The season of waiting could be the season when you are expecting something; a child, financial breakthrough, etc. The season of harvest could be the time of business and career expansion, childbirth, etc. If you are in any of these seasons, you will need to ask yourself, "What are the most important things needed for this season?" You may identify three basic needs required for that season; it might be two or even one. Carry out this evaluation for different aspects of your life: Ministry, career, business, social impact, etc.

Determine the things that you are responsible for.

Once you have identified the most important things, you will then need to go a step further to find out what other things you are primarily responsible for that did not come into your list of the most important things. This is also important because life places certain responsibilities on our shoulders. They may not be as

5. Prioritize the demands of your season

important as the things that will make up for our success, but fulfilling them brings a certain level of fulfillment; hence, they would need to be considered in the equation of balance.

Focus your most productive energy and time on those important things.

This here is so important because it will determine your effectiveness and efficiency in each season. Having identified the most important things for each season, ensure that daily, you are giving your most productive energy and time to them. If morning hours are the best times when you feel most energized, ensure that you put in a significant hour of your mornings into those important things. If it's night that you are most alert and energized, maximize your night hours. My point is to ensure that the times you are allocating to those most important things in your life are the times when your productive energy is at its peak. Don't use your most productive energy and time for your responsibilities and leave out your important matters for other times.

Delegate and supervise some responsibilities.

5. Prioritize the demands of your season

Identify responsibilities you don't have to do by yourself and, as much as possible, delegate them to someone else and supervise them during and after the task has been done. This is crucial as it will go a long way in determining whether you will be successful in creating an effective and efficient balanced life. Many women shy away from delegating responsibilities. Some of the reasons they have for this could span from…

- The fact that they enjoy performing those responsibilities. That you enjoy some things does not mean you must personally perform those tasks.
- The belief that you are the only one who can do that thing to your taste and standard.
- Feeling guilty about giving out responsibility. Sometimes we become so emotionally attached to a responsibility that it becomes difficult to delegate it.
- The thought that when delegated, it will take longer than if you perform it yourself hinders us from delegating.

5. Prioritize the demands of your season

- Lack of trust and confidence in others to perform.

These and many others are the reasons many find it difficult to delegate; however, you must go past these roadblocks and delegate if you must achieve balance as a woman. Delegating responsibilities frees up time and allows you to focus on the most important things that will get you where you want to be.

Let the important people in your life know your priorities for each season as you go through them.

Communicate the priorities of your life with the most important people in your life. These could be your spouse, children, parents, siblings, direct managers, and bosses. Find a way to let them know that this is your focus for this season. If you are in a season when you will need to give more to your career, maybe because of a promotion you want to get, or a learning journey you need to undertake that will make you less available at the home front, let your spouse know, let your children know if they are at the age when they can understand and then, when that season is over, create time make up for the lost time. If you are in a season when you need

5. Prioritize the demands of your season

an opportunity to develop certain skills and experiences at the workplace, speak up; let your managers or whoever holds the key to such opportunities know. If you are in a season when you need to pay more attention to the home front, communicate that to your bosses, especially if you have bosses who support and are rooting for you.

Master the act of saying 'no'.

Each time you say 'yes' to something, there is always something you have said 'no' to. Mastering the art of saying "no" is an important strategy if you will effectively be able to prioritize the demands of your season and consequently achieve a fulfilling life, particularly as a woman who juggles several demands of life at the same time. Saying "No" is not about being rude or inflexible, it's about being purposeful with your commitments to ensure that your energy and efforts are invested in endeavors that align with what matters most for each season of your life. When you say 'yes' to everything and anything, you will be stretched so thin and will have little left to give to the things that matter. Many women end up saying 'yes' to things they want to

5. Prioritize the demands of your season

say 'no' to because of certain reasons, some of which include:

- Other people's perception: Some women end up saying 'yes' to things they should have said 'no' to because they do not want people to perceive them as arrogant or unresourceful.
- The desire to be in everyone's good book: Some accept things just because they want to be in everyone's good book, but you need to realize that no matter how hard you try, you will not be able to please everyone.
- The feeling of guilt: Some feel that when people ask them to do something, they must be in need and they would not have asked if they weren't. Yes, the person might be in that particular need but it must not be met by you.
- Scared to say 'no': Some women are scared to say 'no', especially if this is coming from someone they either respect, or love, or someone with higher authority. Others are also scared to say 'no' if they grew up in a background or

5. Prioritize the demands of your season

culture where they are not allowed to have an opinion.

Now that you understand that you need to say 'no' to some things in order to prioritize the things that give you a sense of fulfillment, how then do you practice the act of saying 'no'?

- Practice 'Pause, think, and Respond': There is always this tendency to want to say yes to every request, but you will need to intentionally practice pausing and thinking through the request in light of the other things you have outlined to do. This reflection ensures that your decision is intentional and aligned with your capacity and priorities at the time.

- Evaluate the Request: Evaluate the request in light of your priorities and responsibilities. Ask yourself if performing that task is enabling your core priorities or will be a distraction from your primary focus areas. For example, if in your office you are asked to volunteer for a cause, however at this season of your career, your focus is on growing your hands-on skill and this

5. Prioritize the demands of your season

volunteering would not contribute to this core focus. You can then proceed to ask yourself if you have the capacity to go for that volunteering, and if the answer is yes, you might decide to then say yes to it even though its not core, but its something you will love to participate in.

- Communicate honestly: Communicate your decision with utmost honesty; appreciate the person requesting you to perform that task or to help or volunteer or whatever it is, then let them know that because you are focusing on a different priority now, you are not able to assist.
- Provide Explanation: If there is a context where you need to provide further explanation as to why you are saying no, please do. This enables people to see from your perspective and maybe, understand. Not everyone will understand, but you have done your part.
- Make Alternative Suggestions: If you can make alternative suggestions for someone else or something else that can be done, do not be hesitant to do so. This will put you in the light of

5. Prioritize the demands of your season

a valuable person and show your commitment to the person making the request even though you are not able to directly assist them.

Chapter Exercise

Reflect on the following questions and write down your answers.

1. What are my current priorities for the different areas of my life? List them.
2. How well have I prioritized the things that matters in my current seasons?
3. What adjustments do I need to make?

CHAPTER SIX
MASTER THE ACT OF SELF-MANAGEMENT

In every mathematical equation, you will have constants and variable parts of the equation that determine the outcomes. The constants cannot be altered; hence, if you want to alter the outcome, you will need to adjust the variables of the equation. Since time is a constant, what you do within the time you have are the variables that can alter the outcomes of your life, hence the concept of self-management

6. Master the act of self-management

Many people seem to emphasize time management but, I like to replace time management with self-management. Every human being on Earth has 24 hours every day. It is a constant resource given to all people on the face of the Earth, irrespective of skin color, race, gender, belief system, geographical location, or season. It is the same amount of time that we all have, so I always think about time as a constant in the equation of life. In every mathematical equation, you will have constants and variable parts of the equation that determine the outcomes. The constants cannot be altered; hence, if you want to alter the outcome, you will need to adjust the variables of the equation. Since time is a constant, what you do within the time you have are the variables that can alter the outcomes of your life, hence the concept of self-management. Therefore, self-management is important for a woman who wants to achieve stability and fulfillment in life.

Self-management is the ability to manage your behaviors, thoughts, and emotions consciously and productively. It is managing yourself, and aligning your

6. Master the act of self-management

activities in a manner that ensures optimization of your most productive energy and time. Self-management means you understand your personal responsibilities, roles, and needs in different aspects of your life and seasons, and you do what needs to be done to accomplish them in the most fulfilling way.

A woman with strong self-management skills knows what to do and how to act in different situations. For instance, she knows how to control her anger with a co-worker when unduly provoked, and how to manage relations with spouse, friends, parents, and kids in a way that ensures she maximizes the benefits from those relationships. She knows how to avoid distractions while working from home so she can maintain focus and stay productive. She knows what she needs to do to achieve her goals in every season and she follows through with plans.

Self-management is only possible for a self-aware woman. To be able to manage yourself, you need to understand your strengths, weaknesses, opportunities, seasons, and the specific challenges and setbacks. Only

6. Master the act of self-management

with that understanding can you begin to control and express them appropriately.

Why is Self-management important?

From the perspective of a woman who wants to be effective and attain balance, self-management skills are critical, especially with the many roles and responsibilities we are faced with daily. Self-management is crucial for regulating our behaviors, making sound decisions, and ultimately enhancing our lives.

Skills that will increase your self-management capabilities:

Clarity

For self-management to be possible, you will need clarity—clarity about what matters most to you, clarity about your seasons, clarity about your roles and responsibilities, clarity about the direction you want your life to take, clarity about the demands of each season, and clarity about how to get there. Have you ever found yourself moving around aimlessly or

6. Master the act of self-management

repeatedly engaging in tasks only to realize in the end that you haven't accomplished anything? This often happens when there is a lack of clarity about your objectives.

I recall a situation from the early years of my career when I was assigned a task. I thought I had clarity on what needed to be done. However, after spending the entire day on it and presenting the result to my manager the next morning, he realized that I had approached it the wrong way, and the outcome was not as expected. This experience taught me a valuable lesson about the importance of clarification. It taught me to seek clarity before embarking on any endeavor, whether at work, in business, in ministry, or in any other area. You need to ask yourself these questions:

- ➢ What exactly am I trying to achieve? The aim of asking this question is to clarify the purpose and objectives of your actions.
- ➢ How does this align with my current season and priorities? This question aims at ensuring that

6. Master the act of self-management

your efforts align with your long-term and short-term goals.

- ➤ How can this be achieved? In answering this question, identify the tools and resources that can facilitate your efforts most effectively and efficiently.
- ➤ How can success be measured? Define criteria for success to gauge your progress and determine if your objectives have been met.

Strategic Planning

Another essential skill for self-management is strategic planning. You need to step back and envision the big picture of your life. What do you want to be known for in your workplace, family, business, and every other aspect of your life? Your big picture may include the legacy you wish to leave behind. This forward-thinking approach allows you to start working towards your future today, focusing your commitments, efforts, and energy on achieving your long-term goals.

6. Master the act of self-management

Setting Priorities

Once you understand what needs to be done, prioritize tasks to ensure goal achievement. By tackling the most important tasks first, you can effectively manage your responsibilities and avoid being overwhelmed by competing demands.

Regulation of your Emotions

Being aware of our feelings is paramount to regulating them. At every point in time, various emotions and feelings are going on within, the feeling of anxiety, fear, amusement, contentment, guilt, shame, fear, etc. They may not all be happening at once, but at different times we must have experienced one or more of these feelings. A person who has built Self-management capacity will need to be aware of her feelings, and then regulate them in such a way that they do not hinder her productivity. It could be an emotional feeling of not being competent enough, the fear of failure, the anxiety that comes with raising kids, the contentment of staying in an old season and not striving for a higher level, etc, but a woman who

6. Master the act of self-management

has mastered herself will navigate through these emotions and channel them appropriately, directing the positive ones into achieving her goals and working through the discomforts of the negative ones.

Self-Care

The only person who can truly be responsible for caring for you is you. Balance will be elusive for you as a woman if you do not take the time to take care of yourself. Many women carry the ingrained belief that serving others, taking care of others, and sacrificing oneself at the expense of taking care of others and things is a noble cause, however, you need to understand that you need to be whole to take care of others effectively and efficiently. We need to understand that we need to be at our best to do our best and that if we don't practice self-care, we have unconsciously reduced our capacity to contribute to others' welfare. Taking care of yourself includes taking care of your health, and your spiritual, mental, physical, and financial well-being.

6. Master the act of self-management

Take care of your spiritual needs, and spend some time with your maker. The more you can connect inwardly, the more you can be equipped to take care of every other area of your life.

Take care of your health, don't focus on the well-being of others at the expense of your own health. A story was told of a woman, who loved her job so much that no matter what's going on in her life, she must be there. She often placed her job above every other thing in her life. She often missed doctors' appointments because she needed to be at one business meeting or the other. This went on year after year, and she later died of a terminal illness that was not detected on time. Even before her demise, her position at work was already given to another. You must understand that once your health is gone, you will not be able to achieve anything. So, prioritize taking care of your health. Take enough water, eat right, and exercise regularly as these all add up.

Take care of your mental well-being. Taking care of your mental well-being could range from productively

6. Master the act of self-management

engaging your mind, reading, and removing yourself from relationships and situations that constantly push you low mentally. It could be something as simple as making connections with people who speak words of encouragement and spur you to be the best version of yourself and cutting away from those who bring the least out of you. It could be something as little as reading for thirty minutes every day and spending an extra five minutes meditating. It could be having some me time where you relax your mind and have some good rest, not thinking about how to take care of something or someone else. You may be surprised how refreshed you would be after those sections. If you have had a long stretch of hours working and taking care of others, take out a couple of days and have a proper rest. Many women go months and even years without finding time to rest. Don't do that to yourself.

Focusing on what you can control

No matter how good the plan you make, or how well-organized you are, there are certain times and things that will be outside your control. Part of the skills you need

6. Master the act of self-management

to build as you grow in your self-management capacity is focusing on the things within your control. One of the things within your control is your response to people and the things around you. You will not always have control over other people's behavior towards you, but what you can control is your response to their actions. You may not have control over the policies and bills made by the government, but you can decide the actions you take to be in a better place despite the impact that policy could potentially have on your business. You may not be in control of how your spouse or children may behave but what you sure do have control over is how you choose to respond to those happenings.

Creating time to have meetings with yourself

Socrates once said that an unexamined life is not worth living. How will you know the progress you are making in your life if you don't make evaluations? Every serious organization usually has meeting times when they evaluate, and make plans, and as the year progresses, they also have review meetings where they evaluate the plans they have made versus the actual. In

6. Master the act of self-management

the same manner, you might have had your goals set and seen the big picture of your life, but periodically, you will need to take inventory of your life and evaluate how far you have gone to determine if there are places where adjustments need to be made and if there are there habits stopping you from actualizing the future that you have seen. Are there new opportunities that you were not initially aware of when you made those plans that you need to consider now? These and many more are the things you do when you call yourself to a meeting. Do not run your life without regular pauses and check-ups. More so, schedule the time for this meeting, don't assume that it can happen when it happens because more often than not, it will not happen. In the same way you plan for everything, take some time to plan for the meeting with yourself. Be honest in your meeting with yourself, give accolades to yourself on the things you have achieved, and as well, tell yourself what has not gone well and take the steps to make it better going forward.

6. Master the act of self-management

Self-Nurture

Invest in your personal development by acquiring new skills and knowledge that can enhance various aspects of your life.

Practice Patience

Self-management is a skill that takes time to develop. Be patient with yourself, learn from your experiences, and keep practicing to improve your competence over time.

Chapter Exercise

Reflect on the following questions and write down your answers.

1. Do I have clarity about different areas of my life
2. How well have I prioritised self-care?
3. What adjustments do I need to make

CHAPTER SEVEN
BALANCING ART

Balancing life is more of an art, and just like an artist creatively finds a way to pull his imagination into a physical reality, you will need to continuously evaluate your life in each season and creatively find a way to achieve balance.

7. Balancing Art

The famous scientist Albert Einstein once said that Life is like riding a bicycle and to keep your balance, you must keep moving. In the same way, life is like a machine with several moving parts, never constant, always moving, therefore, to keep balance you must engage all its moving parts, probably not at the same rate and time but each part must be engaged. For example, in a car, the different parts are engaged, the engine, the kicks, the gear, and every part of the car is involved in ensuring the car is moving and gets to its destination. If any critical part that ensures the car's mobility gets dysfunctional, the car will not move, no matter how effective the other parts are. Similarly, if your life will be effective, you will need to build balance in all the critical parts of your life. To keep your balance, you must keep moving, you must keep rediscovering the mix of strategies that work best for your specific purpose and need.

Balancing life is more of an art, and just like an artist creatively finds a way to pull his imagination into a physical reality, you will need to continuously evaluate

7. Balancing Art

your life in each season and creatively find a way to achieve balance.

Balance will not mean that everything will go the way you planned. Things will sometimes not go your way. Unexpected events will sometimes show up. Your boss will add a new meeting to your busy schedule, new projects will sometimes creep in unplanned, a sick family member may require your attention, or a friend might call you at the last minute for urgent assistance. What will help in those times is your adaptability to the moment rather than the rigidity of sticking to plan.

I have therefore drafted below, some of the strategies that could help you in improving your life balance as a woman. You can begin by implementing one at a time or a couple of them at the same time and after you've mastered the ones you've chosen, begin to incorporate the others. Remember that finding an approach that works for you is a process that will take time.

Determine what you want to be remembered for.

Every builder always starts with a building plan, and that building plan is where the builder determines whether the building would be a bungalow, a three-story

7. Balancing Art

building, or a skyscraper. As much as having the right resources/opportunities is important, knowing the desired result of the combination of the resources/opportunities is more important. Imagine using up resources that could build you a skyscraper to build just a bungalow. This can only mean that a lot of those resources were wasted. Why? It's because you didn't understand 'what' you were trying to achieve. In this case, it was not a matter of having the right resources, neither was it a matter of know-how, it was a matter of not defining 'the What'.

To arrive at balance will require you to start with the end in view, 'The What' of your life. When all is said and done, when you will be leaving this earth realm to transit into the world beyond, what will you be remembered for? In your family, what do you want to be remembered for by your spouse and your children? Do you want to be remembered as that spouse and mum who created quality time for the family? In your career/business, do you want to be remembered by your colleagues, your bosses, and clients as one who gets things done without throwing others under? What social

7. Balancing Art

impact do you want to be remembered for; what communal impact do you want to be remembered for? In your ministry, what impact do you want to create in the lives of others? You need to outline all the important areas of your life and answer the question of what.

Define what is very crucial if you will rightly arrive at the mix that makes up your balance every year, month, day, and even hour. It will help you determine the opportunity cost, the activities you will be willing to give up when there are competing tasks that require you to make a choice.

It is also important to mention that this is not a one-time evaluation, It is something you keep doing as life unfolds. This is because, at the beginning, things may not be so clear but with each passing season and time, the vision becomes clearer, and you keep redefining and expanding on 'The What'.

Evaluate where you are currently.

You then need to evaluate where you are in relation to 'The What' you have identified. 'The Where' defines how far you are in achieving that set 'what'. How far

7. Balancing Art

are you from achieving 'The What' in family, career, business, ministry, social impact, etc?

Realign your current state to reflect the long term.

The essence of evaluating 'the where' is to determine if you are anywhere close to your set objectives or still far away from them. The result of this evaluation is what necessitates the process of realignment. Realignment is not a one-time event, it is a process that you perform every day, every month, or every year. In your journey to balance, you must schedule moments of reflection when you think about your current state in relation to what you are trying to achieve. In the same way you schedule your daily tasks, schedule a time of the day, month, and year when you will have reflection moments to ask yourself these important questions:

- What area(s) of my life am I invested in right now?
- Is this area aligned to the long term?
- What has been working?
- What has not been working?
- What are the most common obstacles?

7. Balancing Art

- ➢ Am I sacrificing too much of the other areas in other to meet the demands of these focus areas now?
- ➢ What things, relationships, or systems do I need to put in place to ensure that the other areas are not suffering while I'm focusing on this/these area(s)?

Remember that the goal is to ensure that you have the right mix of activities, and engagements that ensure a balanced and fulfilled life, so you don't want to be so fixated on one area and the others suffer massively. Therefore, even though you are focusing on an area, you are also ensuring that you are making the right amount of deposits in the others to keep them afloat and functioning.

Set times and honor them.

Time is a limited resource that needs to be maximized and used prudently. Therefore, it is important that you carefully evaluate what you are spending your time on especially given the unlimited needs and wants they will need to be allocated to. A woman who must achieve balance must set out time for things she wants to achieve

7. Balancing Art

and honor them. If you set out time to spend with family, honor it, if you set out time to meet up with a task in your career, honor it, if you set time to meet with your connections, please honor it. This is why it's so important that before you fix those times, you have to carefully consider all the other things you have to do. Yes, some uncertainties might come up but if you have been a person that has been honoring time, it will be easier for people to understand when those unpredicted circumstances come up. In the case where anything comes up, be sure to communicate this to the persons involved.

Set healthy boundaries.

Boundaries differ from person to person and will differ from culture to culture. Boundaries will also differ in context. Boundaries appropriate in a business environment will most likely not be important in a home setting or any other type of environment, hence it is important to set healthy boundaries for the different kinds of relationships and context you might be involved in. Setting healthy boundaries defines our expectations of ourselves and others.

7. Balancing Art

Setting healthy boundaries requires you to be self-aware. You are conscious of your strengths, and limitations. It will also require you to clearly communicate those expectations. When communicating these expectations, you will need to be clear and assertive.

Pay attention to your tasks.

Whether they are tasks you have personally assigned to yourself based on your personal goals or tasks based on the roles you play at work or home, you need to pay attention to them. Paying attention to your tasks ensures that you are giving them the best of your energy and achieving a worthwhile result. Do not just go through the day being absent-minded from the tasks you have at hand. Perform them within the allocated time.

Pay attention to your connections.

As human beings, we are all built for meaningful connections. In a particular study conducted by Dr. Holt-Lunstad, She explained that humans need to be socially connected as a part of our neurobiology, which can shape how we think, feel, and behave. When our social needs are not met for a sustained period, there

7. Balancing Art

will be dysregulation of our biological systems which can lead to the development of diseases.

What then makes up a meaningful connection; Is it the number of people you know? Is it your perception of closeness to other people or is it the number of quality relationships you have? The answer according to Holt-Lunstad, Robles, & Sbarra, 2017 is that it is a combination of all of these. Having many connections, especially in this age of social media does not equate to a meaningful connection. In fact, studies have shown that loneliness in the U.S. was increasing before the pandemic and has increased over the past two years. According to a 2021 national survey by Harvard researchers, 36% of respondents reported feeling lonely "frequently" or "almost all the time," 61% of them were young people aged 18-25, and 51% were mothers with young children. This increasing number does show that despite the large number of connections on various social media platforms, the malaise of loneliness is still a major issue.

7. Balancing Art

When it comes to building connections, our goal is not simply to meet more people and increase the number of connections we have. Our goal is to find the people that make us feel really good about ourselves, less lonely, and well-supported. In building healthy connections, we must put in the effort to make the most of our relationships, so that they stay strong and healthy. Make time to have quality connections with your spouse, children, extended family members, friends, and colleagues.

Family: From your busy schedule, create time to have meaningful conversations with your spouse. For your children, depending on their age, there are seasons of their lives when quantity equals quality. Those are the times when they are much younger, and you will need to spend that time with them however as they grow, you will need to have meaningful conversations with them. You may need to explain why you might not be there all the time but whenever you are there, be there, make it a quality time; find out what is going on with them, don't be with them and you are doing so many other things. Occasionally plan vacations together with your spouse

7. Balancing Art

and children and build memories together. These are the memories that will keep the relationship and make up for the times you may not be there. For those who feel close to their other families (Siblings, parents, etc)—or want to feel closer—it can be worth making an effort to talk more often. Even if you live far away, you could schedule a phone or video chat with them.

Friends and colleagues: Developing and strengthening personal connections with friends and colleagues does not just happen, it takes time, emotional intelligence, and many a time, financial commitment. Therefore, you will need to be intentional in selecting these connections. In terms of friendships, you will need to know why you are keeping those friendships. Is that friendship enabling you and the person to become more of who you ought to be? If yes, are you investing the right amount of time, energy, and resources to nurture that relationship? Ask yourself, is there a friend you would like to spend more time with? Is there a colleague that seems nice who you'd like to get to know better? Have you been making the right investment in those connections? When I say investment, it's not just

7. Balancing Art

money, it includes time, kindness, emotional support, support with skill, and others.

Community: Community can be an important meaningful connection. Personally, I have been able to achieve certain things that I could not do personally just by connecting to a community with the same objective. I remember after giving birth to my second daughter, I was struggling with committing to a routine of exercise to lose some of the post-partum weight. I joined a community of women who were having the same struggle and I saw massive results within one month. Connecting with a community can enable you to achieve some things that you may not be able to achieve on your own. It could be a professional community, a spiritual community, a family community, a community of people that enjoy similar hubby, etc. In choosing the community to join, ensure that you are guided by your life vision and your short-term goals.

Connect with God: Whether you are religious or not, the truth remains that human beings have a source and for me personally as a Christian, I believe that our source is God. The times when I have felt my life so out

7. Balancing Art

of balance have always been when I don't feel that connection with Him.

A meaningful connection with your God can contribute massively to your ability to maintain a balanced life. Connection with God gives you a sense of direction, it realigns you when you start going off your path, and ensures that you have the right wisdom that guarantees fulfillment. Without that connection, no matter the level of success you can achieve in any other area of your life, you will always have a sense of something missing.

Connecting spiritually With God will involve spending some time in prayer, and His word, scheduling time for meditation, and spending time in prayers. It will also require connecting with others who share similar beliefs with you as a way to build community and practice together. Books and messages also go a long way in maintaining that connection.

Find the mix that works best for you and your purpose.

Finally, your balancing art will always require that you find your own rhythm, your own mix of strategies that works best for you. Design a strategy that works best for

7. Balancing Art

you and the people in your life. Re-evaluate as seasons change. Your life will constantly evolve, and as that happens, you will keep adjusting to suit, keeping your eyes on the big picture of your purpose; 'The What' of your life.

Chapter Exercise

Reflect on the following questions and write down your answers.
1. What area of my life do I currently feel most out of balance?
2. Why do I feel out of balance in this area?
3. What adjustments do I need to make?
4. What connections, boundaries, etc do I need to adjust to ensure I bring balance to that area

CHAPTER EIGHT
INTEGRATE LIFE

Integration fosters a mindset that considers the big picture, evaluates the various components contributing to it, and synergizes their interaction.

8. Integrate Life

Over the years, the concept of compartmentalization in life has been admired by those striving for effectiveness in various areas. This approach involves mentally separating work, family, social life, and other aspects into distinct compartments, and dealing with each separately. While this method may seem effective for managing energy and focusing on individual tasks, it can lead to negative consequences if not monitored in the long term. Many who adopt compartmentalization may discover later that they've focused excessively on one area while neglecting other crucial aspects. Billy Graham, a renowned international evangelist of the mid-to-late 20th century, was undeniably successful in ministry, yet on his 90th birthday, he expressed regret for not spending enough time with his family.

Creating compartments can provide organizational structure but may inadvertently lead to neglecting essential parts of life, potentially causing a collapse in the long run. I recall a scenario in my own home: in an attempt to organize my kids' clothing and belongings, I designated compartments in their wardrobe for different

8. Integrate Life

items. While this helped with organization, it caused me to overlook certain items in certain compartments. I found myself using items that were more visible and easily accessible, leading to a cycle where frequently used items were washed, sorted, and reused while others languished in the compartments, eventually becoming obsolete as my kids outgrew them without utilizing them.

Similarly, we might become so absorbed in work that family time is neglected, or so focused on ministry that we overlook our family's well-being or our own health. We could also be deeply involved in community impact to the detriment of our career, business, or family.

Life integration, on the other hand, involves blending different aspects of life. Life is an integrated unit, much like the elements that make up an atom. Your life purpose is the big picture, but different facets of your life come together to fulfill that purpose. Integration fosters a mindset that considers the big picture, evaluates the various components contributing to it, and synergizes their interaction.

8. Integrate Life

Integrating life allows space for every important aspect, ensuring that none is neglected for too long, thus enabling holistic success. While the idea of blending all aspects of life may seem daunting, it need not be overwhelming. Establishing a new system begins with evaluating your current rhythm, systems, seasons, and strategies, and determining their effectiveness for you.

Define your specific goals for life integration.

While it's an overarching approach, life integration varies for different individuals and seasons of life. For instance, integrating life when your family is young might involve dedicating both quantitative and qualitative time to family while progressing in your career or business at a slower pace. It may mean reducing social engagements to focus on professional growth without neglecting other aspects. Building support systems can also be integral during periods when you're less available in certain areas of life. Define what will harmonize the different parts of your life, considering not only your needs but also those of the important people in your life.

8. Integrate Life

Identify and Maximize Your Resources.

Integration is not achieved in isolation; rather, it's attained by identifying and maximizing the resources available to you, enabling the integration of various aspects of your life. These resources could encompass human support, technological access, financial means, and more. The human resources may include supportive friends, a supportive spouse, understanding extended family members, colleagues, employees, or employers. Integration without people can be challenging; therefore, you need support from people important in your life. For example, securing support from your spouse is crucial. The choice of a life partner is significant; therefore, marry someone who aligns with your vision, understands your specific needs, and is committed to standing by you every step of the way.

Supportive friends and family can provide stability, offering assistance with childcare, emotional support, and more. Likewise, employers who prioritize your well-being are invaluable. They weigh in with flexible work arrangements, focusing on productivity rather than fixed office hours, allowing for a better balance

8. Integrate Life

between family and work responsibilities. I can count the number of times I've had to juggle between family and work. This was possible because I had employers who were willing to be more flexible with work arrangements, considering productivity and results rather than insisting on fixed criteria of being in a fixed office to do my job.

In addition, If you have people you employ to work under you, treat them with respect and appreciation for their contributions to achieving your goals. Value them and never take them for granted.

In today's era of advanced technology, maximizing available tools is essential. From the invention of phones in the 1800s to today's smartphones and tablets, communication has evolved drastically. Utilize technology to facilitate constant communication and streamline tasks through various apps and tools. The goal is to leverage technology effectively to enable seamless life integration.

8. Integrate Life

Identify your current rhythm and update them.

Your rhythm has to do with your Routines, Emphases, Structures, Pace, Interconnections, and Ideologies (RESPII).

In music, rhythm is a regularly repeated pattern of sounds or beats used in songs, poems, and dances. It brings synchronization. In the same vein, your rhythm is your regularly repeated pattern which has formed a habitual way of life. Identifying your current rhythm will help to evaluate your life and identify areas that need a total overhaul, and areas that need to be improved on in order to bring sync to your life. Let's drill down to discuss the various elements of rhythm as applicable to the subject matter of integrating life.

Routines:

To effectively integrate life, you need to identify your current routine and then evaluate if this current routine is working in a way that brings effectiveness and efficiency. Routines are the repeated actions you take on a daily, weekly, monthly, or even yearly basis which at some point, have become a part of you, such that you do them without giving so much thought or energy to

8. Integrate Life

them. Establishing a routine creates a flow for life. Imagine waking up tomorrow and not knowing what you will be doing. Chances are that you will wake up to nothing, not knowing what to do. Inversely, if you have a routine already, it will be easier to wake up and fix other things that come up during the day. Routines can make life easier to integrate, it's like having a system, where every unit knows what, when, and how they are supposed to operate. So, think about your already established routines like waking up in the morning, having time with God and meditating, preparing your kids for school (if that is the season you are in), going to work, having specific times when you do your laundry, specific days when you handle your finances within the month, specific time for family, me time, specific time of the year when you go for holidays, etc. These sorts of routines kind of help to reduce the friction and chances that some areas or some things will not be attended to. Look at the things you have been doing repeatedly for the past 3 months that have formed your routine, and ask yourself how well are they serving you in integrating every important aspect of your life.

8. Integrate Life

Identify routines that have become repugnant, and remove them. Identify a new set of activities that will help you integrate and incorporate them into your routine. If for example, you are already a busy working mum, incorporating a family time where on a daily or weekly basis you are able to put off distraction and focus on activities that help you bond with family. This may seem like a little action but it can make a difference and ensure that you are integrating your family life into your whole life.

Your emphases:

Every season of your life will have specific emphases. In a particular music, certain keynotes and words stand out, those are the emphases that produce that specific rhythm. In the same way, seasons of your life will need you to emphasize certain things and certain activities. In your journey to a balanced and integrated life, you will need to identify those emphases and make them pronounced in your routine without necessarily losing sight of the other areas of your life. I will also want to emphasize that effective integration and balance will

8. Integrate Life

require that you are sensitive to know when there is a shift in emphasis and adapt your life to match the shift.

Your structure:

Similar to routines is your structure. Your structure has to do with the systems you have put in place to ensure that you are maximizing life. Your structure includes the way you have organized your routines and your emphasis. It has to do with the way you have structured your systems of support.

Your pace:

This has to do with your speed. Some seasons of your life will require that you slow down on some areas of your life and increase your acceleration in other areas. If you are a woman who wants to achieve balance, you need to pay attention not just to the things you are doing but the pace at which you are doing them. It is important to highlight here that you are not in competition with any other woman, so avoid the temptation to compare your life with others'. Move at the pace you can handle at a time. Move at your own pace, do not allow the society or socially-defined pace to define the pace of your life. In my life, I have seen career women who

8. Integrate Life

pursued career advancement at a great speed and others who took their time to get to the limelight. They all got a sit at the table. At the top, no one is asking them how long it took them to get there, the main thing is that they all got there and are contributing their quota on the table. This is just a simple example of moving at your own pace in terms of career. It can be in terms of any other area of your life; marriage, having kids, ministry, etc. The point here is not staying in the path of least resistance but moving at a pace you can handle that effectively allows you to integrate every aspect of your life and ultimately when all is done, you can look back and say you made the best use of all that was available to you in those seasons.

Your Interconnections:

In looking at the rhythm of your life, you will need to look at the interconnection of your life. What makes music and rhythm come out beautiful is the interconnections of the notes; how beautifully the different notes are linked and connected in such a way that what comes out of it is pleasing to the ear. In the same way, if you must succeed in integrating life, you

8. Integrate Life

will need to identify how different aspects of your life are interconnected and also, ultimately connected to your purpose as a person. For instance, if your job brings out your communication and soft skills, which you are able to utilize for ministry or for any other social impact, that will be a motivation to keep improving on those skills not just for the purpose of work but for the social impact and happiness you derive when you do those things. If you have kids and are able to develop some level of patience, empathy, and strength that can also be applied at work, that can be a drive to continue being a great mum. These are just a few examples. Someone can take it a step further to ask, "Does being at work bring a sense of purpose such that I feel that am doing something impactful and fulfilling?" It is this sense of purpose you derive from work that provides you the needed energy to function more effectively at the home front, ministry, and other areas of interest outside work. The interconnection could also be that with the finance from your career or business, you are able to fund your family life, social impact, and other

8. Integrate Life

dreams that you may not be able to afford if that career or business is taken out of the equation.

Identifying the link/interconnection to the different aspects of your life is absolutely important to be able to integrate life at its core. It is what will keep you pushing when the chips are down. It will help you persevere when it seems like all is falling apart.

Your Ideologies:

At the core of every rhythm produced, are the ideologies. Your ideologies are what back up your rhythm. Your ideologies are the set of ideas, beliefs, and principles on which your life is hinged. Sometimes, we are unaware of these ideologies because we have not premeditated on them. These ideologies get ingrained into our subconscious based on culture, past experiences, and exposures.

If you grew up in a family where your mum and all the women in your family were very keen on pursuing career progress, there is a high tendency that you will be keen on pursuing the same path. If you grew up in a home where your mum was a stay-at-home mum, chances are that you will likely stay on that path. If you

8. Integrate Life

grow up in a society where hard work is rewarded, chances are that you will want to work for everything you get. Ideologies back up our decisions when life presents us with choices.

In the discourse of integrating life, your ideologies will determine whether you will even make the choice of integrating life or sticking to what you have known that may not necessarily allow you to achieve much success with your life. As a way to move forward, you will need to examine those ideologies. You will need to revisit your ideology of what being a successful woman should look like, your ideology of work and hard work, your ideology of raising a family, and your ideology of how these different areas of life integrate. Ask yourself if these ideologies have become sabotaging and are limiting you from achieving true success and fulfilling your life purpose and if they are not, what do you need to intentionally start changing? Mind you, ideologies don't change overnight, it will take intentionality. How? At every point when you need to make a choice, ask yourself what ideologies are sponsoring these decisions, if you have a different ideology based on who you want

8. Integrate Life

to become at the end of your life, would that decision be different? Then, make a decision different from what you would have done if you had not premeditated on that decision. With every alternative action you take rather than the default one, you will gradually be replacing those ideologies.

Check In Constantly!

Integration of life is not a one-time thing. This is because life changes in the long term. Life is not a constant equation; at some point, some elements of the equation will change without even seeking your permission and because of this, you need to check in with yourself constantly. Check that your life is being integrated in the way you want it and that it is still in shape with your big picture. Checking in can be done biannually, annually, or even once in two years, just so it does not become too burdensome. During your checking-in, you are asking yourself how the different areas of your life that make up your core are faring, is there any important area of your life that like my kids' closet scenario we discussed at the beginning of this chapter, that has been left unattended to? What

8. Integrate Life

adjustments do you need to make sure that you integrate this(these) area(s)? It could be changing your rhythm, utilizing your resources, etc.

Chapter Exercise

Reflect on the following questions and write down your answers:

1. What are my goals for life Integration?
2. What resources are available to me to achieve my defined goal?
3. What are my current rhythms?
4. What adjustments do I need to make to this current rhythm?

CHAPTER NINE
GRIT AND ADAPTABILITY

Fostering adaptability requires developing a futuristic perspective, recognizing that you have control over your choices, being planful, and actively engaging in an ongoing process of wisely evaluating courses of action.

9. Grit and Adaptability

One key strategy a woman who wants to experience balance and fulfillment in life must deploy is the development of grit and adaptability. Grit is a concept that allows one to tenaciously pursue a course with both passion and perseverance in the long term (Duckworth et al. (2007). Adaptability, on the other hand, refers to the ability or willingness to change in order to suit a changing environment or situation. These two traits are absolutely important for a woman in her journey of balance. Life is ever-changing; our environment, personality, and circumstances are always changing. Sometimes, unplanned events that can destabilize your plans, and an entire system and structure you have put in place happen. Some examples of these changes, whether good or bad, could include losing a loved one, especially those that have been amongst your strong support system, losing a job, relocating to a different area or a different country where you have no system of support, getting a new job in another industry, a breakdown in health, or maybe, just recovering from an ailment and just trying to get back your life together,

9. Grit and Adaptability

increase in responsibility both at home and work environment, having a new baby, etc. Any of these life changes can happen to anyone.

Nearly all changes, whether good or bad, are stressful and require adaptability to manage successfully. Fostering adaptability requires developing a futuristic perspective, recognizing that you have control over your choices, being planful, and actively engaging in an ongoing process of wisely evaluating courses of action. Regaining focus and balance after a change has happened will require great grit and adaptability, it will require your active involvement. On the other hand, the alternative is passivity and reactivity. Sitting back and just letting things happen takes less effort, but it is the recipe for disappointment and an unhappy ending.

In my life, I have seen these concepts of grit and adaptability make a difference between champions and losers. I have seen people who actively choose to do what it takes to come out stronger from situations that break many. For the sake of privacy, I'll withhold their real names.

9. Grit and Adaptability

The first story is about Rose. Rose was in a very committed relationship, or so she thought. However, a few days before her wedding, the young man called it off, citing incompatibility. It was a difficult and messy breakup. Instead of actively taking steps to heal and move forward, she chose to passively dwell on the past, waiting for her ex-partner to re-initiate contact or for the situation to magically resolve itself. This led to prolonged feelings of sadness and stagnation in her personal life. She couldn't find closure, which prevented her from having any fruitful relationship afterward. She always came across as bitter and carried this bitterness into subsequent relationships.

In another case, there's Emily. Emily had been working in the administration of a company for over a decade. She was comfortable in her role and enjoyed the stability it provided. She could be said to have been one of the best administrators anyone could have during those years; she was skilled at her craft. However, with the passing years, her industry began to change rapidly due to technological advancements, and her skills became obsolete. Instead of proactively seeking

9. Grit and Adaptability

additional training or exploring new career opportunities, Emily chose to remain passive, hoping that her experience alone would be enough to sustain her career. As time went on, Emily's job became increasingly insecure as younger, more tech-savvy professionals entered the workforce. Despite warnings from colleagues and industry trends indicating the need for upskilling, Emily hesitated to take action, fearing the unknown and clinging to her familiar routine. Eventually, Emily's company underwent a major reorganization, and her position was eliminated. Suddenly faced with unemployment, Emily realized she had been too passive in managing her career. She struggled to find new job opportunities that matched her outdated skill set, and the financial strain began to take its toll. However, this setback served as a wake-up call for Emily. She enrolled in courses that will update her skills, networked with professionals in her field, and embraced a proactive approach to her job search. Despite the initial challenges, Emily eventually found a new position that not only utilized her existing experience but also allowed her to grow and thrive in a

9. Grit and Adaptability

rapidly evolving industry. Through this experience, Emily learned the importance of being proactive and adaptable in the face of change, and she emerged stronger and more resilient in her career journey.

These two stories demonstrate the need for one to actively adapt and build grit in the face of change and challenge. While these traits may come naturally to a few of us, for the majority, they need to be cultivated.

Strategies for building grit and adaptability:

Strong Sense of Purpose

Purpose, according to Stacey M. Scheafer, is finding meaning in your life. It is discovering reasons to keep pushing forward regardless of the circumstances life throws at you. A strong sense of purpose greatly improves your ability to adapt to different phases and areas of your life. Draft a strong sense of purpose for different areas of your life: your marriage, career, ministry, social life, and health. Allow me to say that if you do not find a reason that is intrinsically driven, you may find it difficult to move forward when changes shake the core fabric of your existence. If all your sense

9. Grit and Adaptability

of purpose is externally driven, when those external factors phase away or change, you will find it difficult to cope. For example, if your sense of purpose for work is only driven by praise and recommendations from others, what happens when those are not forthcoming? You will find it hard to stay on top of your work. If your marriage is driven by how great your spouse looks or how you feel around them, what happens if something happens to how they look or how you feel? If your ministry is driven by only the positive outcomes, what happens when those results may not pour in as you expect? Let me tell you what might happen: you might lose the grit to stay through to the end.

Commitment to Upholding Desirable Values

Values are the principles upon which life is built, serving as the bedrock for individuals and nations that have achieved significant progress. Whether intentionally identified or not, everyone operates based on a set of values. Among these values are the very critical ones such as integrity, patience, love, empathy, contentment, generosity, perseverance, and appreciation for family life and growth.

9. Grit and Adaptability

To identify the values you operate with, consider the attributes that have influenced most of your decisions in the past three to six months, whether at work, home or in the community. Can you pinpoint the persistent ones? These are the values upon which your life has been based. Then, ask yourself whether these values align with the purpose you defined earlier. If they do not, consider drafting a new set of desirable values to drive your life. Every time you need to make a decision or take action, let it be guided by these defined values.

Embracing Challenges and Discomfort

When faced with challenges and unexpected changes, we are presented with opportunities that can either strengthen us or leave us feeling broken, beaten down, and lacking belief in ourselves. What determines whether we emerge stronger or broken is our acceptance of the transient nature of these challenges. Recognizing that these circumstances are not permanent but merely passing phases is crucial. Understanding that while challenges may bring great pain, they also offer significant opportunities for growth can profoundly

9. Grit and Adaptability

impact our mindset when navigating life's unpleasant turns.

Accepting challenges and discomfort provides the necessary energy for creativity. Challenges can propel us to a place where we begin generating ideas and contemplating the actions needed to overcome them. You've likely heard the saying that challenging times birth the greatest inventions. The same holds true in our lives; we, as women, can choose to allow the challenges we face to inspire greatness within and around us, or we can passively observe events unfold.

Moreover, embracing challenges can enhance our mental flexibility, enabling us to navigate obstacles more effectively. This openness allows us to discover new paths toward our goals. Sometimes, the absence of challenge and comfort can lead us to become fixated on specific steps to achieve our objectives, closing us off to unexpected opportunities that may lie outside our plans.

Achieving a better balance involves evaluating the challenges we encounter. When going through a

9. Grit and Adaptability

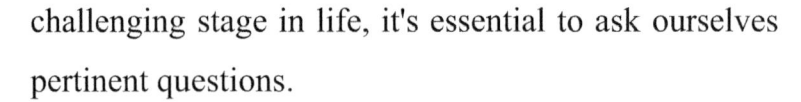

challenging stage in life, it's essential to ask ourselves pertinent questions.

- What will I learn from this challenge?
- What opportunities can I see from them?
- How do I maximize the opportunities?

Getting creative in challenging times, evaluating opportunities in relation to your goals, and getting used to being uncomfortable all help you to accept more challenges. The more practice you have at this, the easier it becomes to find and embrace new opportunities in life. Over time, you will be able to build more capacity to handle more challenges and develop more empowering beliefs that will support you through any challenge that life throws at you.

Deliberately Choosing Your Response!

The truth is that you do not have the power to control all that happens in your life. There are certain things we do not have control over, but there is one thing we all have a choice on; it's our response. Yes, you didn't make the choice to get sick, but you can choose to be happy, you may not have made the decision to break up with the person you were in a relationship with but you

9. Grit and Adaptability

can choose how you react to it afterward. You can respond by being bitter and unforgiving, you can as well decide to dust yourself up and live a happy life. You may not have planned to lose a job, but if it happens, you can choose to upskill and apply somewhere else. The bottom line is that you have the capacity to choose your own response. You may not have the capacity to choose other people's actions and how they react to you, but you can choose your response. And as a guide, choose happiness; choose what brings out the best in you, what brings you inner peace and joy, what makes you sleep well at night, and something which at the end of your life, you can look back with no regrets.

Being Optimistic About Your Outcomes

You are the greatest cheerleader of yourself; therefore, to be energized enough to carry on that role to the end, you must see beyond your current challenges and trying situations. You must envision a great outcome. Challenging situations and obstacles are a part of life. When you're faced with one, focus on the good things, no matter how small or seemingly insignificant they may seem. Always look out for them, and you will find

9. Grit and Adaptability

them. You know the popular saying that you can always find the proverbial silver lining in every cloud — even if it's not immediately obvious. Once you find that outcome, be thankful for it. Focus on that great thing, that creative outcome, rather than the pain of the moment. Focus creates blindness; when you are focused on the great outcome, it can become the drive to push through to the end.

Giving birth to a baby is one of the most difficult and painful experiences women go through, but have you wondered why most women endure the process? It's because of that inexplicable joy that comes when you carry the baby in your arms for the first time. It is this outcome that keeps women pushing throughout the nine months and during childbirth.

The joyous outcome of an athlete crossing the finish line with the awards, medals, and accolades that accompany it — those are the visions that keep them pushing through the rigors of practice and training.

If you want to develop your gritty ability and adaptability, then you must see an optimistic outcome for every season, every challenge, all turns, and tussles

9. Grit and Adaptability

of life. You must see a light at the end of the tunnel if you will develop the grit and adaptability required to reach that end.

Taking and Growing from Baby Steps

There are three categories of women you will find: those who are passive, not taking any steps because they are either afraid to take any steps at all or afraid of failure if the steps fail. Sometimes we don't even take the first step because our dreams, goals, and desires seem so overwhelming, so big, and seemingly unachievable that we give up before we even start.

The second category consists of those who attempt to take too many steps at the same time. In this age and time where we are all in a hurry, we want everything now; happiness now, success now, health now, love now. Not surprisingly, many women attempt to make life changes and face challenges in the same way.

The last category comprises those who take gradual but progressive steps. This has proven over the years to be the most effective way to build anything lasting in life, whether it's career advancement, building a business, improving fitness, organizing habits, nurturing

9. Grit and Adaptability

relationships, or sustaining a marriage. This may be the simplest, yet the most effective strategy we can use to build consistency, adapt, and eventually live a life of balance and success.

I have watched my kids move from being babies who could not hold up their necks or any part of their bodies. At those stages, you literally have to support them in every part of their body because they are fragile. Gradually, they learn how to hold up their necks, then they start learning how to sit, crawl, and stand. In the next stage of their development, they learn how to take their first steps. The stronger those steps get, the more they are able to take other steps, and eventually, they start walking. But you know what, from the time they were born, all of that potential was inside of them!

In the same way, you will not know your level of grittiness until you start taking those baby steps. The happiest and most successful people will tell you that they have achieved their level of life and work success by taking small steps and making one positive choice after another.

9. Grit and Adaptability

The more you experiment with those baby steps, baby ideas, baby thoughts, and baby actions, the more you will develop your ability to handle greater responsibilities and challenges that life throws at you.

Embracing Discipline as a Way of Life

No one achieves anything significant in life without a measure of discipline, including becoming gritty and adaptable. Discipline is a powerful tool that empowers you to make life choices that align with your goals, values, and aspirations. It's about making decisions that support your overall well-being, enabling you to navigate through life even when they require effort and commitment.

Many times, discipline comes off as strict routines and denying yourself certain pleasures. However, when reframed to mean committing to consistent actions that propel you towards your goal and proving to yourself that you believe in your potential and are willing to invest in your growth, it makes a lot of difference. Discipline nurtures a deep sense of trust and respect for yourself. When you commit to yourself and stay true to

9. Grit and Adaptability

your promises, you reinforce the belief that you can create positive change. This trust becomes the foundation upon which you can build a gritty and adaptable self-image.

Living Mindfully

Mindfulness is being present as you go through life. It means thoughtfully engaging yourself as you go along on the journey of life. When life challenges happen, you can decide to live in the past, or shield yourself from the world and life in your head or you can decide to embrace living in the present and taking actions that can lead you to a greater future. We will dive more into this in the next chapter.

Chapter Exercise

Reflect on the following questions and write down your answers.

1. What challenges have I faced in the past and how have I navigated through them?
2. Based on what I have learned from this chapter, what could I have done better?

9. Grit and Adaptability

3. Write down actions to take going forward to improve your adaptability.

CHAPTER TEN
EMBRACE MINDFULNESS AND PRESENT LIVING

In practicing mindfulness and present living, you will need to pay attention first of all to yourself, secondly to your connections, and thirdly to your environment in the now

10. Embrace mindfulness and present living

Many women float through life without actually engaging with it; they just watch weeks turn into months, and months into years. I experienced this at certain seasons of my life until the realization dawned that life is meant to be actively engaged with, not passively floated through.

A story was shared privately by a woman called Sonia (this is not her real name, but for the purpose of this discussion and privacy, let's call her that). Sonia was a career-driven woman in her late twenties, working in a fast-paced corporate environment. She prided herself on her ability to multitask, juggling numerous projects and deadlines with ease. By her late twenties, she was already married with kids. Although she attended to her responsibilities as a mother when she could, she didn't realize the minute details of her young children's lives she was missing out on. She didn't realize how far apart she was growing from her spouse and kids. Although she felt her professional and family life were moving on smoothly, Sonia often found herself overwhelmed and stressed, but she didn't really mind because she believed that it was all part of life.

10. Embrace mindfulness and present living

Fast forward to 2020 when COVID-19 happened and the world seemed to stand still. Companies closed their premises and operated more online. Sonia took some of those weeks during COVID-19 to take some of her overdue vacation. Because schools were also shut down, Sonia had to find ways to spend quality time with her kids. During those months spent at home, she noticed some of the details she had missed in her kids' lives. She realized how much less time she was spending with her spouse and how much less time she had been spending with her family. It took COVID-19 to make her pause and think deeply, to realize that life was beyond having a busy work life. It took COVID-19 to make her realize how stressed she had been from prolonged working without taking intermittent breaks. From then on, she started incorporating simple practices into her daily routine, such as taking short breaks, paying attention to the sensations in her body, paying attention to her kids and spouse, and paying real attention to her environment. As she became more mindful and present, Sonia noticed a gradual shift in her outlook on life. She began to appreciate the small

10. Embrace mindfulness and present living

moments of joy and beauty that she had previously overlooked, even in those chit-chats with her kids.

Her story exemplifies the lives of many women today, especially in a fast-paced world where we are constantly either overemphasizing the future or worrying about past errors. Many women are preoccupied with thoughts about the next promotion, the next big news, the next breakthrough, or the next world uncertainty, such as the wars already ongoing in different parts of the world, high interest rates, high cost of living, high energy prices, etc. It is no wonder that different women go through this bustling life without enjoying the small details and beauty of the present. Therefore, we need to consider mindfulness and present living as critical aspects for women who want to achieve balance and truly enjoy fulfillment.

Mindfulness and present living involve focusing your attention on the present and paying attention to the happenings around and within you. To be present in the now, you must not allow worry about the future or the past to deprive you of the joy of today. In practicing mindfulness and present living, you will need to pay

10. Embrace mindfulness and present living

attention first of all to yourself, secondly to your connections, and thirdly to your environment in the now.

Pay Attention to You

Paying attention to you means paying attention to your Spirit, soul, emotion, and body. Paying attention to you is critical in your journey of balance. It takes a wholesome you to achieve balance and a wholesome you is achieved when you are operating optimally spiritually, mentally, emotionally, and in your body.

Your Spirit

You need to pay attention to what goes on in your spirit. I believe that we are spirits possessing a soul and living in a body. To therefore achieve mindful living and ultimately balance, you need to pay attention to what happens in your spirit. Some of the ways I have learned to connect to my spirit is to shut myself out from external noise; noise in my environment and noise in my head. Learning to be still and calm is the springboard upon which you can connect spiritually. This is particularly important, especially in a world with so much external noise. When you are able to focus within

10. Embrace mindfulness and present living

and focus on your source (God), you are able to draw much strength and energy for every other area of life. Other things you could do to connect to God include;

- Communication with your maker. Some call this prayer, but for me, this is all about talking to God and Him talking back to you. When you speak to him and listen for what He has to speak, He speaks back to you through the voice of your spirit (heart).
- Studying spiritual materials that help to build you up spiritually.
- Listing to that small still voice within.

Your soul

Pay attention to what is happening in your soul. Paying attention to your soul means paying attention to what is happening with your emotions, your mind, your feelings, and your choices. When your soul is healthy, what will proceed from it will be joy, peace, compassion, trust in God's goodness, creativity, gratitude for the things you have and for the people around you, generosity toward others, a clear sense of vision, intimacy with others, energy for work and other

10. Embrace mindfulness and present living

areas of life, and a strong desire to connect with God. However, when your soul is unhealthy, you will generally feel frustrated, discontented with life, bitter, fearful, ungrateful, restless, and all the other negative emotions that flow from it.

In your journey of mindfulness, a direct pointer to what is happening in your soul is the emotions, thoughts, and choices that flow out of it. So, spend some time today and ask yourself what exactly is going on within your soul. A healthy soul always springs from one that is connected and receptive to God.

Your body/health

The next aspect you need to pay attention to is your body and your health. To function optimally on Earth, your body needs to be catered for. That's why it's essential to pay attention to your body. Recognize when it's time to take a break, rest, and rejuvenate. Self-care is part of taking care of your body. Paying attention to what you eat and exercising your muscles are also essential parts of taking care of your body.

10. Embrace mindfulness and present living

Paying Attention to People

Up next is paying attention to your connections; the people around you. We are built for relationships, and cannot exist or function effectively alone, that is why relationships matter; so, pay attention to them. Some of these important connections include your spouse, kids, parents, siblings, friends, colleagues, and your community.

Your Spouse

Pay attention to your spouse if you are married. Your spouse is an important part of your life and your journey, so you need to pay attention to him/her. Share your experiences and also validate their own experiences and emotions. Communicate the priorities of your seasons to your spouse as you go along in life and ensure that they are carried along every step of the way.

Your Kids

Pay attention to your kids as they go through the various seasons of their own lives. Do not be absorbed in your own world and fail to recognize and guide your kids as

10. Embrace mindfulness and present living

they go along in their own seasons. Validate and support them as they navigate their paths.

Your Family and Friends

Pay attention to your connection to family and friends. By family here, I mean parents, siblings, and extended family members. Life can be more colourful when you have very supportive family and friends and if you are fortunate to have one, pay attention to them, nurture and grow those relationships, and do not take them for granted.

Your Colleagues/Worker

If you happen to be an employee, chances are that you will have people that you work with, and if you own your own business, there will be people working with you. This set of connections can play a vital role in enabling you to achieve your goal, hence you will need to pay attention to this connection. Treat them with utmost respect and create the right values and boundaries that will allow this relationship to thrive.

Your Community

As a woman, I cannot begin to emphasize the importance of a community. You need a community of

10. Embrace mindfulness and present living

people with similar values and interests, hence you will need to pay attention to this. Be intentional in connecting with and maintaining this community.

Paying Attention to Your Environment

You need to pay attention to your environment. Many times, we miss out on the beauty of life when we do not pay attention to our environment. Dozens of research show that paying attention to our natural environment has lots of benefits, such as increased cognitive ability, promoted happiness, improved mood, and mental well-being.

One such study was conducted by Alison Pritchard, PhD, at the University of Derby in England. She found that people who feel more connected to nature experience a type of contentment that goes beyond just feeling good; it includes having a meaningful purpose in life (Journal of Happiness Studies, online first publication, 2019).

In a modern world generally characterized by busyness, people often do not pay attention to what is happening in and around them. This has been further exacerbated

10. Embrace mindfulness and present living

by the sense of connection people establish on various social media platforms, pulling the average person further away from paying attention to their physical reality and environment. Therefore, it is important that in our journey of balance and mindful living, we pay attention to our environment and the happenings around us. Take some time to appreciate the natural creations around you: the blue sky, the sun's brilliance, the beauty of the moon, the presence of birds, and the well-structured buildings. Notice the artwork in your living room and admire its craftsmanship.

The point is to take some time out of your day to step away from overthinking about the past or the next course of action and simply enjoy the moment. Enjoy yourself, enjoy the people around you, and appreciate the beauty in your environment. In this way, you will begin to feel a sense of satisfaction that emanates from within, a peace that flows from your spirit to your soul and permeates every aspect of your life.

10. Embrace mindfulness and present living

Chapter Exercise

Reflect on the following and write down your answers.

1. How Healthy is my Spirit, soul, and body?
2. In what ways can I improve my connection with people?
3. What actions can I take every day to focus on my environment for a few minutes daily?

TIEING EVERYTHING TOGETHER

What have we learned about balance for a woman juggling different aspects of life?

Tieing Everything together

Congratulations! You have stayed through to the end. It's now time to tie together a few things we have learned from this book. This chapter is a bit of a summary, a few short and actionable lessons to enable you to achieve balance as a woman.

In the intricate complexity of a woman's life, balance is not a static state but a dynamic journey, one that requires continuous adjustment, reflection, adaptability, and grit. In this book, we have explored the various seasons a woman's life goes through which makes it more complicated for her to find balance since each season has its own peculiarities and demands. As we conclude, let us take a step back and look at a few guiding principles.

1. Embrace your seasons:
   The more we struggle to accept the seasons of our lives, the harder it becomes to achieve balance or any sense of fulfillment,

regardless of our activities during those seasons. A young mother who struggles to accept the season of raising children will constantly feel frustrated and inadequate, regardless of the sacrifices she makes. A young woman in the season of growth and exploration may face an identity crisis if she has not accepted that she is still in the process of self-discovery during this season. The first step is to evaluate the current season of your life and mentally note your acceptance of it.

2. Determine the priorities of each season:

Every season has its priorities and key demands. Therefore, your focus should be to ensure that the primary aspects of each season are attended to. For other areas that are not crucial during that season, implement systems to ensure that they are monitored and not neglected. It's akin to juggling balls: you focus intently on catching the ones closest to you without losing sight of those farther away. While these distant areas may not be the season's priority, neglecting them could cause the entire juggling system to collapse.

3. Acceptance of Imperfect days:

   Perfection is an illusion that often leads to unnecessary stress and disappointment. Accepting that there will be days of imperfection allows us to appreciate our efforts and achievements without the burden of unrealistic expectations. It's important to recognize that balance does not mean doing everything perfectly but doing what is most meaningful and fulfilling to you.

4. Prioritize Self-Care:

   Self-care is the foundation upon which all other aspects of life are built. It is not selfish but essential. Prioritizing physical health, mental well-being, and emotional stability equips us to face life's demands with grace and strength. Remember that you are a key

Tieing Everything together

factor, a key element in the equation of balance.

5. Set Boundaries and expectations:

   Clear boundaries are vital for protecting your time, energy, and well-being. Learn to say no without guilt and delegate tasks when possible. Boundaries help maintain a healthy separation between work, personal life, and every other in-between of life, ensuring that none consumes others. Clarify people's expectations of you and be clear about your own expectations of yourself.

6. Foster Supportive Connections:

   Surround yourself with a network of supportive friends, family, and colleagues. These relationships provide a safety net, offering encouragement, perspective, and assistance when needed. Do not hesitate to lean on your support system; human connection is a powerful tool for maintaining balance. Your important connections could help you to achieve things that are important to you in each season.

7. Practice Mindfulness:

   Staying present in each moment of life can enable you to focus without the unnecessary distractions from regrets of past mistakes or worry about the uncertainties of the future. Focus on the health of your spirit, soul, and body in the now, the important connections you have in the now, and what is going around you now.

8. Embrace opportunities for personal and professional development.

   Adaptability and a willingness to learn can transform challenges into stepping stones toward a more balanced and enriched life.

9. Reflect and Reassess:

   Regular reflection helps you stay aligned with your values and goals. Reassess your priorities periodically and make necessary adjustments. What worked at one stage of life

Tieing Everything together

may need re-evaluation as circumstances change. Flexibility is key to sustaining balance over time.

Finally, balancing a woman's life is a deeply personalized journey, unique to each individual's circumstances, dreams, and aspirations. It requires a harmonious blend of self-awareness, intentionality, and compassion. By embracing these principles, you can navigate the complexities of life with confidence and poise, creating a fulfilling and balanced life on your own terms.

Acknowledgements

Like all books, the book '*Balance*' would not have been possible without the help and the support of countless people who have helped and supported me along the way. There are too many to list them all. But a few who have been particularly supportive:

My husband, Franklin Ojukwunze, you are the most supportive husband anyone could ever wish to have. Thank you for partnership and friendship.

Paschal Ugwunso: Thank you for your encouragement and painstakingly editing this work.

Osiri Favor: Thank you for encouraging me to write at a point I was delibrating on whether to write or not.

Benjamin Dike: Thank you for being a great mentor, thank you for challenging us to maximize every platform we find ourselves.

Colleagues and Bosses: You all make balancing work and the in-betweens of life possible.

Friends and family: You have been my strong support system, thank you.

Printed in Great Britain
by Amazon